read

BooksM
Family h
FaxingG

Please
avoid f
person

24 hou

Bletcl
King
MK (
New
Oln
Story

796363925

Fernando
TORRES

Fernando
TORRES

LIVERPOOL'S
NUMBER 9

Ian Cruise

MILTON KEYNES LIBRARIES		
MKC	DON	6/12
796.334 CRU		

JOHN BLAKE

Published by John Blake Publishing Ltd,
3 Bramber Court, 2 Bramber Road,
London W14 9PB, England

www.johnblakepublishing.co.uk

First published in hardback in 2009

ISBN: 978-1-84454-731-9

All rights reserved. No part of this publication may be reproduced, stored in a
retrieval system, or in any form or by any means, without the prior permission in
writing of the publisher, nor be otherwise circulated in any form of binding or
cover other than that in which it is published and without a similar condition
including this condition being imposed on the subsequent publisher.

British Library Cataloguing-in-Publication Data:
A catalogue record for this book is available from the British Library.

Design by www.envydesign.co.uk

Printed by CPI William Clowes Beccles NR34 7TL

3 5 7 9 10 8 6 4 2

© Text copyright Ian Cruise 2009

Papers used by John Blake Publishing are natural, recyclable products made from
wood grown in sustainable forests. The manufacturing processes conform to the
environmental regulations of the country of origin.

CONTENTS

PREFACE

'He's certainly made life tough for the foreign boys coming to England now... no one now can make excuses about needing time to settle.'

Those were the words of Liverpool captain Steven Gerrard just seven months into Fernando Torres' first season at Liverpool, and it's easy to see where he was coming from when he made that statement. Put simply, Torres' impact on English football in his debut campaign was nothing short of remarkable.

After all, Gerrard is exactly right in what he says. It's often stated that it takes a player several months to settle into life at a new club. With players coming into the Premier League from abroad, it has long been accepted that the first season will be a bedding-in period – almost a period of grace – while they get used to the pace of English football. Torres, though, made a mockery of those suggestions during an unforgettable first season at Liverpool in which he broke records galore and won a permanent place in the hearts and minds of the Anfield faithful.

If it's possible to go from nowhere to legend status in just nine months, then Fernando Torres has come as close as anyone to achieving that. Almost from the first moment he set foot on the Anfield turf, it was clear that he had found his spiritual home.

Atletico Madrid will, surely, always be the club he calls 'his team', having grown up idolising his heroes at the Vicente Calderon Stadium and having achieved his boyhood ambition of playing for his home-town club. Not only that, he was their youngest-ever captain and the talisman for a team and the sporting organisation as a whole.

Atletico, however, despite their lofty aspirations, could not offer Torres the biggest stage, the one his talents truly warrant. For that he had to leave Spain; for you could scarcely imagine him pulling on the shirt of either Real Madrid or Barcelona, the only two clubs in his home country that could offer him the elevated platform on which to perform. That would have felt too much like a betrayal of 'Atleti'.

Instead, by choosing to move abroad, he has been able to fulfil his ambitions far enough away from Madrid for all his successes not to cut like a knife among the Vicente Calderon diehards, who can now watch on with immense pride as one of their own continues to blossom and develop into one of the world's most feared forwards.

And in Liverpool, he found a team, a club, a city, perfectly in sync with his own psyche – the passion of the region reminds him so much of the fervour that surrounds Atletico Madrid; and, among those who make the Kop one of the most vibrant stands in world football, he has found a multitude of kindred spirits. They, in turn, have welcomed him as one of their own.

His goalscoring feats spoke volumes in his first campaign at Anfield, louder than any words ever could, but the supporters were quick to let him know how highly they regarded him in their affections. Within a few short months of his arrival on Merseyside, the Kop was jumping to the sounds of the 'Fernando Torres Song'. To the tune of 'The Animals Went In Two By Two', tens of thousands of voices could be heard chorusing:

> *'His armband proved he was a red, Torres, Torres,*
> *You'll never walk alone it said, Torres, Torres,*
> *We bought the lad from sunny Spain,*
> *He gets the ball, he scores again,*
> *Fernando Torres, Liverpool's number nine.'*

The armband it refers to was one he sported during his Atletico days, though the actual words on it were 'We'll Never Walk Alone'. Although it's true he was a Liverpool fan from afar, the words also refer to a bond he shared with his boyhood friends. As a symbol of that bond, his friends all had the words 'We'll Never Walk Alone' tattooed on to their arms, something that Torres, as an Atletico Madrid player, clearly could not do. The captain's armband, with the inscription on the inside, was his way of showing his solidarity with his mates.

For Liverpool fans, though, the words were enough to prove his loyalty to them and the song was born... and it's a song Torres adores.

He told Spanish TV station TeleMadrid at the end of his first year at Anfield, 'The song still sends shivers down my spine. It's an unbelievable feeling when you hear the fans singing your song. There are times when I hear it like 20 times during a game. I don't know how the fans can get behind a player in that way, and in such a short space of time.'

The Liverpool fans could probably answer that one quite easily. They, and supporters everywhere up and down the country, find it easy to adopt a new hero once he has proved his worth on the pitch, and Torres was clearly doing that. From the first moment – when he truly broke into the consciousness of English fans as he skipped past Chelsea defender Tal Ben Haim as if he were not there, then slotted the ball past Petr Cech on his Anfield debut – it was obvious that the record transfer fee Liverpool had paid to secure his services would prove to be worth every penny.

Supporters and pundits alike could see that the young Spaniard was, undoubtedly, the 'real deal'. Legendary Anfield goalscorer Ian Rush was particularly impressed with the way he opened his Premier League goal account against José Mourinho's Chelsea side. The Welshman said after that match against the men from Stamford Bridge, 'Torres couldn't have done any more to win over the Liverpool supporters against Chelsea. His goal reminded me of a young Michael Owen, with lightning pace and a perfect finish. When you have a striker with that kind of speed, it's a major asset for any team. But just being fast isn't enough – you need to be quick off the mark to make the most of your qualities, and, if you add the kind of awareness and finishing ability we saw [against Chelsea] into the mix, it's some combination.'

And it was a combination that was to unsettle Premier League defences everywhere as he took the English game by storm. He netted hat-tricks in the Premier League against Middlesbrough and West Ham, as well as against Reading in the Carling Cup, and his record of 24 league goals in his debut season was the most ever recorded by a foreign import in his first campaign in English football's top flight.

Not that his success should have taken people entirely by surprise. This is a man who, at 14, was named the Best Player in Europe for his age group by a panel of UEFA officials. Such accolades are not heaped lightly on such young shoulders, but Torres has always demonstrated the capacity to cope with those pressures. He scored winning goals for Spain's junior teams in both the Under-16 and Under-19 European Championship finals and performed admirably as the focal point of a largely under-achieving Atletico Madrid side.

His former Atletico Madrid youth coach, Pedro Calvo, never had any doubts that the young man under his wing would go on to become a global superstar one day. On the eve of Euro 2008, he told the BBC's website, 'I always knew he'd make it as a professional. I never had any doubts. In fact, I still have an article that was published in the newspaper *Marca* when we were about to compete in the European tournament after winning the Under-14 Spanish Championship title. We had a young team with many boys who later became world-famous players and I had always said that, if Fernando continued to progress, he would achieve similar success.

'He has always been surrounded by coaches, such as myself or Abraham Garcia, the current coach of Atletico Madrid B. We have always tried to guide him in the right direction. Fernando always accepted help and advice. He analysed everything we told him in order to make the right decisions. And he has always been a very intelligent player, always level-headed when it came to making important decisions.'

And it was a combination of his abilities and that intelligence that convinced Calvo that Torres was making the right decision to move to England when he finally decided the time had come to quit Atletico Madrid.

'Because I know him both on a personal and professional level, I think the English league, above the Italian and Spanish leagues, was the best choice for Fernando,' he continued. 'So I'm not surprised as to how quickly he has adapted. I think that some Atletico fans assumed he would take a little more time to settle. Even in England, I don't think people expected him to start as well as he did. But I think Liverpool manager Rafa Benitez is still expecting a lot more from Fernando in years to come. He's obviously helped him adapt quickly and he doesn't have the same sort of responsibility that he held at Atletico, like being named captain when he was only 18, and carrying the weight of an entire club on his shoulders. Fernando is an incredible player with the potential to change the face of football. I believe that he will continue to improve and go on to achieve even greater success.'

Torres' commitment to his craft is absolute and he works extremely hard honing and perfecting the skills that make him one of the most lethal finishers in world football today. It's also likely that his prodigious work rate was inspired by a couple of sportsmen he has named as being among his boyhood idols, former US basketball great Michael Jordan and legendary Spanish cyclist Miguel Indurain, who became the first man ever to win the Tour de France five times between 1991 and 1995.

Talent alone, however, is not the only secret to Torres' success, it would appear, for, like many sportsmen, he also has a superstitious side to his character that comes to the fore when he is on a hot streak. 'I'm very manic', he admitted in an interview with UEFA's *Champions* magazine. 'I once combed my hair into a crest because a friend suggested it and from that moment I started to score goals. I always repeat what I did the day before a game if I've scored. So if, when I score, I've stood up on the coach on the way to the game, I'll stand up again. If I've spoken to someone, I'll speak to them again. I always repeat it. But my main characteristic is willpower. So far I've achieved everything I've wanted. I'm lucky, but nobody has gifted me anything. Luck is important, but you have to go out and get it. I've always admired people who have achieved what they have through their talent.'

Whatever his secret – or whatever his superstitions – his methods clearly work for him. From idolising the likes of Jordan and Indurain as a kid, his waxwork model now stands alongside theirs in a Madrid museum, taking pride of place along with other footballing legends of the city like Raul and Zinedine Zidane.

That is an honour that makes his father, José, immensely proud. He says, 'It's only a few years ago that I used to take him to training and he made the jump to the [Atletico] first team. Now, I can't believe he can have come so far, so young.'

It certainly has been an incredible journey, but in many ways it is a journey that is only just beginning. Victory with Spain at Euro 2008 was his first major honour and he has spoken passionately of his desire to add to that, with both club and country. Liverpool came close to European glory in the Champions League in his debut season, but lost out over two legs to bitter rivals Chelsea in the semi-finals, a defeat Torres described as a 'nail in my heart'. And he and his team-mates know that domestic championship success is long overdue for the Anfield club.

'My dream is to win a title with Liverpool', he told *FootballPunk* magazine on the eve of the 2008/09 season. 'I have been very fortunate with Spain and enjoyed the best moment of my sporting life when we won Euro 2008. So I know what it feels like to win a major trophy. Now I want to experience the feeling with Liverpool'.

If he is able to help the club achieve their first ever Premier League title success, Fernando Torres' legacy at the club would surely be cemented for eternity. But one former Anfield hero reckons he doesn't necessarily needs a cupboard full of medals to make sure of his place in the upper echelons of the club's illustrious hall of fame. 'For a player like me, who sat just behind the strikers, Torres would be an absolute dream to play with', says former England great Peter Beardsley. 'I really wouldn't be surprised if he goes on to become a Liverpool legend'.

1

EARLY DAYS

Fernando Torres was born in Madrid on 20 March 1984, the third child for his parents, Flori and José. His brother and sister, Israel and Mari Paz, were seven and eight respectively at the time of his arrival into what was, by all accounts, a lively household. Well, with three small children on the loose, how could it be anything else?

It was not long, however, before the young Fernando – or 'Nando', as he has become known to many – was channelling his energies into developing the skills that would later make him one of the most feared goalscorers in world football. In fact, he was just two years old when he first began to show off his ball skills, kicking elder brother Israel's football around the house. Imagine that – barely old enough to be walking unaided and already playing football. Maybe the ball at his feet somehow helped his balance. Whatever the reason, it must have been apparent from an early age that he had a special talent for the sport.

One can only hope, though, that, as his football talent blossomed, so his financial awareness improved along with it. One of his favourite childhood tales concerns one of his much-loved boyhood hobbies – throwing things out of the window! On this particular occasion, however, the model truck he chose to launch into space was full of money, and soon that cash was being scattered on to one of Madrid's streets, much to Mum and Dad's consternation.

By the time the young Fernando was four, football had grown from a small child's hobby into something which, while not quite an obsession, was certainly more than simply a passing fancy. He would spend hours on family holidays in Gastrar, a small village in Galicia, kicking a ball around with his father. There was no real structure to their play, no rules, they simply enjoyed having fun together. And, at that stage, Fernando would have settled for that. At four, he had little idea of pursuing his favourite pastime as a career.

His first experience of organised football in a structured environment came when he joined his first team in 1989, at the age of five. They were called Parque 84 and their first tournament was in a 'footballathon' at the local sports centre in Fuenlabrada. The event lasted two whole days, manna from heaven for the football-crazy youngsters. Not that there was a great deal of shape to their play in those early days. Fernando recalls on his official website that 'the matches consisted of 15 to 20 kids running around after a ball... really crazy! Nonetheless, for a kid like me at that age it was a big deal.'

By the time he was six, football had become really important to him. It's not clear, though, quite where his love of the game comes

2

from. One of the abiding memories from his childhood, however, was talking to his granddad who, although not a particularly keen follower of football, prided himself on his devotion to the local club, Atletico Madrid.

Fernando recalls, 'My granddad was a strange case in terms of football. The truth is it hardly interested him, but nonetheless he was passionate when it came to Atleti. The image is still fresh in my mind of my granddad in front of me, talking without stopping, trying to get across to me the importance of being an Atletico Madrid fan.'

To emphasise his point, Fernando's grandfather gave the youngster a plate as a gift. It had his granddad's name on it, alongside the Atletico Madrid badge. To this day, Fernando describes it as being 'the best trophy I've got'. It would prove to be the first of many.

A slightly more surreal influence on him in his younger days was a Spanish TV cartoon series, *Oliver y Benji*. The story told of a group of young lads who started playing football just for fun, but ended up as professionals. It was a show that clearly had a profound effect on the six-year-old Fernando. As soon as the show had finished, he and his brother would race outside to play football and imagine themselves becoming professional players. Who knows, though, how the striker's career might have turned out were it not for a childhood accident that altered his footballing future for ever.

In those early days, young Nando enjoyed nothing better than playing in goal. That was until the day he had a couple of teeth knocked out by the ball when making a save and that was to prove the end of his fledgling goalkeeping career. There will be many goalkeepers around Europe who will rue the day that incident occurred – subsequently, Fernando's mind settled on scoring, rather than stopping, goals.

On that day, though, a young striker was born and it was as a forward that he joined his second team. A neighbourhood café had assembled a side, 'Mario's Holland', and Fernando was chosen for selection, even though he was younger than the league's official limit. But such trivial matters were not allowed to stand in the way of a youngster and his passion for football... particularly when that youngster proved to be such a lethal weapon in front of goal.

Fernando flourished in this new environment and spent three years playing indoor football in a proper league. Around this time, his dream of becoming a footballer really began to flourish as he learned how to become part of a team, relying on team-mates for help and support and similarly seeing how they relied on him. It was a key time for him, and one during which he matured as both a person and a footballer.

At the age of eight, the Torres family moved house, to Estorde, in Galicia. It was to be a move that would have a profound effect on young Fernando's personal and professional life, because it was there that he met Olalla, who would be his childhood sweetheart and who remains his partner today.

But it was not just Olalla who shared those youthful days with him in Galicia; many of the people he counts as friends today grew up with him. The close-knit support of friends and family has always been important to the home-loving Fernando, and remains so to this day, even though he is now a global superstar earning his living in a foreign country.

Of course, back in 1992, there was little thought of fame and fortune, or of playing football for one of Europe's most famous clubs in what is widely regarded as the best league in the world. In those days, it was all about playing for enjoyment, and casually developing the skills that would one day take him to the greatest sporting arenas in the world. And perhaps it was his first taste of the rarefied atmosphere of a world-class stadium that may have added to the young Nando's drive for footballing greatness. It was on a memorable day in 1993 when Torres made his first visit to the Vicente Calderon Stadium, the home of Atletico Madrid. For the wide-eyed Fernando, like many who push through the turnstiles of a great stadium and see the lush green playing surface for the first time, it was a day full of wonder and excitement.

He was just nine years old on that unforgettable occasion, full of excitement as he pestered his father to tell him where they were going on their big adventure together. His dad, though, probably just as excited as his son about their day out, was keen to keep their destination a secret for as long as possible. But that day, when the young Fernando got to visit the Atletico trophy room for the very first time and see for himself the major prizes he had previously glimpsed only in photographs, was one he would never forget. He'd heard his family talk about them, of course, the World Club Cup, league trophies, the cups that Atleti had won, but that day he got to see for himself.

From that moment on, Fernando began to harbour dreams of life as a professional, playing in the famous red-and-white stripes of Atletico Madrid, and he did not have to wait long before taking his first steps on the path to what would be a road paved with success and glory. At the age of ten, he joined his first 11-a-side team, Rayo 13, and began to get his first taste of what 'proper' football was like. It was no longer simply about having a kick-about with his mates, all frantically chasing the ball and trying to emulate their heroes. Now, it was starting to feel like it was for real.

What was certainly for real was the fact that, at the end of the season, Rayo's three best players would be offered the chance of a trial with Atletico, with a view to joining the club's youth set-up. Young Fernando banged in 55 goals in that debut season for Rayo 13 and, unsurprisingly, was one of the trio of excited youngsters to be chosen for a trial. On the day of the trial itself, he was full of nervous energy and excitement, but things went well. And so it was that, at the age of 11, Fernando joined Atletico's most junior team. The dream was beginning to take shape.

He has fond memories of his early days with Atletico, particularly the training regime under Manolo Rangel, his first professional coach. Whether the time spent with Rangel in those early days could really be termed 'coaching sessions', however, is perhaps open to debate, given that, by Fernando's own admission, 'training was a game, and the matches were fun. That was the part of my life when I most enjoyed my football.'

Whether or not you wish to argue the point that the training sessions did not have quite as much order and structure as they may have done at other clubs schooling boys of a similar age, there is no doubting the impact Rangel's influence had on the youngster. Fernando later said in an interview in *Champions* magazine, 'I've had a lot of coaches, from when I was five, but my first professional coach was Manolo Rangel at Atletico and he was the first one who told me I was going to play in the top flight, but he also used to remind me I should always aim to enjoy myself. He used to let us choose the training exercises, one player each day. He'd ask one of the kids, "What do you want us to do today?" Over the years, you forget the details, but the thing he taught me that has stayed with me is the importance of enjoying yourself, as if it wasn't a job. I learned from him that you have to apply yourself every day in training but, above all, that this is a game to be enjoyed.'

Shortly after joining Atletico, the boys went on a tour to Belgium. It was Fernando's first overseas trip and he remembers being overwhelmed by everything – the hotel, his team-mates, the whole experience – everything about the trip. As he says, 'I was living my dream, or at least that's how it seemed to me back then.'

It was around this point that football began to be the focal point in Fernando's life and the one into which he channelled most energy. Not that he was getting carried away by the success he had had so far – far from it, in fact. But, just like any young footballer taking his first steps on the road to what he hoped would become a professional career he was thrilled to be a part of a club like Atletico Madrid, although he recognised that he still had a long way to go to achieve his dream. He also recognised the part played by his family, and the efforts they made to help him achieve his goals; in those early days, though, it would be fair to say that none of them dared to dream about the heights he might go on to reach.

It's clear that Fernando feels a weight of gratitude to his parents and his siblings for all that his career has brought him. It's a common theme among sports stars who recognise the part played, and the sacrifices made, by their nearest and dearest so that they could enjoy the best possible chance of making the most of their extraordinary talents.

His mother and father both willingly gave up their time and altered their schedules to accompany him to training sessions. His dad was working but would interrupt his day to take the young Fernando to Orcasitas on the train, while at other times his mother would accompany him to the training ground, meaning both a train and a bus ride from home. She did so willingly, without complaint, just to make her son happy. Many mothers of sporting sons can tell similar tales of early mornings and late nights spent on motorways or on various modes of public transport.

That self-sacrifice and determination to give their son the best possible chance of fulfilling his ambitions is something that inspires Torres even to this day, and he fully recognises the importance of the part his parents played during those early years. He has spoken of how all he is now is a tribute to the hard work of his mother and all she gave up for him, and his brother and sister, too, for they also played their part in those formative years, taking their turns to ferry him to and from the training ground. While he honed his skills on the pitch, they sat in the stands studying. There is no doubt that the willingness of his family to put themselves out for the youngster played a vital role in Torres becoming the player he is today. Their support was vital to the progress of Torres as a young footballer.

That Fernando is so free with tributes to his parents says much about his upbringing. And he is happy to share his views on the importance of those formative years with his inquisitors in the media. 'A person is a reflection of his parents. I've never been one for trying to stand out, and I'm embarrassed being the centre of attention, but whenever I am in the foreground, I know my father is always there in the background watching over me,' he told Spanish journalist Guillem Balague in an interview for *Champions* magazine.

It has always been that way. Torres recalled one such occasion when he was playing a junior match for Atletico when he was 11 or 12 years old, and he was substituted by the coach. Throughout the game he had been verbally abused by a man watching the game and he continued his uncharitable appraisal of the youngster as he left the pitch. Remarkably, Torres' father was stood right next to the gentleman in question but did not react in any way. He did not even look at the man. He merely stood there, impassive, not interested in any type of confrontation.

Many parents would have been smarting for a fight, of course, but that was not in the nature of Torres senior. He preferred to support his son with quiet dignity, never mind what may have been taking place around him. And the lesson Torres learned that day was one that has stayed with him throughout his career, and so it is that he is able to ignore the insults and criticisms from people who don't know him.

It is why also he prefers to shun the limelight, especially off the pitch. Just as his father did all those years ago on that day in Leganes, Torres would rather stay in the background, content to let others take centre stage. He added, 'Of course, there have been occasions where I haven't been able to avoid the plaudits, or to be in the headlines, but I have always preferred the people closest to me to get the attention.'

The shy and retiring Fernando may prefer other people to hog the limelight, but it was becoming clear that he would not be able to hide away in the shadows for long, such was his talent and the progress he was making as a footballer during his first year in Atletico's Junior B team when he was 12 years old. It was a difficult season for the youngster and his team-mates, as often they would find themselves up against boys who were older and more experienced and, at that stage in a child's development, that difference in age, however small it may appear to be, can make a great deal of difference in terms of strength and physique.

But, although there was to be no end-of-season title to celebrate, the boys finished in a respectable position in the league table, with much the same side that had played together the year before, so all in all progress was being made. Perhaps the toughest challenge facing Fernando, as it often is for a large number of schoolboy sporting prodigies, was fitting in his schoolwork around his football.

His first full year at the club, 1996, was a memorable one for both Nando and Atletico. Season 1995/96 saw the senior team claim the La Liga title for the first time in 19 years, and they completed a magnificent campaign by winning the Copa del Rey, the Spanish Cup, to claim a fantastic double. For the fledgling striker, the first team's success made his association with the club even more special and he has often spoken of his pride at being involved with the club in those days and, of course, in the days that would follow.

The following year, 1997, he began the season in the Junior A team, now aged 13 and really beginning to appreciate what it meant to be part of a famous organisation like Atletico. He felt a special affinity with the club and its fans even then, and it's one he still shares today. In just a handful of years he had lived through the League and Copa del Rey double, as well as relegation and promotion. He had shared the happiness and disappointment as both a player and a fan, for he still saw himself that way. He had seen just how much the club meant to the supporters, seen them cry tears of both joy and anguish, and even seen them leave the stadium happy despite the fact that the team had lost. They had been glad simply to be there to see their side play. Torres believes that sets Atletico fans apart from those of, for instance, Barcelona and Real Madrid, who are only interested in wining. The Atletico way is more about enjoyment.

Fernando's love affair with Atletico and their supporters was soon to become a two-way street. In 1998, aged 14, he really began to make his mark on a wider audience than those familiar with the junior ranks at the Vicente Calderon. In fact, it was to be a much wider audience. He had already scored 64 goals for the club by the time he was 13, and he would add 68 more over the next two years, establishing a new club record. He also came to the attention of Europe's leading scouts.

His breakthrough from promising local youngster to highly regarded future star came at the European Nike Cup in 1998, a tournament for Under-14s which was contested by many of the leading clubs in Europe, including Real Madrid, Barcelona, AC Milan, Manchester United and Juventus. Atletico won the event and

Fernando was named the best player in Europe for his age group. Quite an accolade for a lad on one of the bottom rungs of professional football's career ladder.

It is an event he remembers with unsurprising fondness, and he also recalls that it was a hard-fought tournament. Atletico enjoyed a memorable 2-0 semi-final victory over their great local rivals, Real, before beating the Italian side Reginna 1-0 in the final thanks to a goal from Molinero. It was the first major medal of Torres' fledgling career and after the event the media began to sit up and take notice of him and interest in him grew – most notably including a reported offer from Arsenal. It was during those days that he started to appreciate what top-flight football was all about and it was something he thoroughly relished.

That same season, he was also voted Atletico Madrid's Junior Player of the Year and it was clear that a professional career, and indeed possible greatness, lay ahead of him. One man had no doubts that he had been watching a star of the future develop before his eyes. Pedro Calvo coached Fernando as a 14-year-old and shaped the side that won both the Nike Cup and the Spanish Under-14 Championship. He had a growing feeling that Torres was special, telling BBC Sport, 'He was one of the best players I had seen in a long time, so I was very excited when I found out I had the opportunity to coach him. And he's the same person now as he was when he was a young boy. He continues to be a player that epitomises teamwork, humility and goodwill. That's why he captained almost all the teams he represented. Then, as now, one of the most important aspects of his game was his pace, in addition to his composure in front of goal.

When most young players, around the age of 13, would get nervous at the crucial moment, Fernando would excel.

'Fernando had great leadership qualities on and off the pitch. Sometimes, footballers learn from their experiences and grow in maturity. Others put their ego first, but this was never the case with Fernando. If he didn't play because of injury, other players missed him. He was often the difference on the pitch, the one who could change the course of a game with his skill and vision.'

In 1999, Nando was faced with a decision he had no trouble making when he was offered the opportunity to sign his first contract with Atletico Madrid. Unsurprisingly, he did not hesitate for a moment. 'I would have signed for life,' he says on his official website. 'When I was a boy playing football with my mates, I always imagined I was an Atleti player. And now I really was one. I was part of the club. I was an Atletico de Madrid player.'

He spent the next year playing for the youth team as he continued his progression and education, with everyone at the club confident he would make the grade and go on to become a first-team regular. But, early in the 2000/01 season, he suffered his first major setback when he cracked a shinbone. It required surgery to correct the problem and meant being sidelined until December. Little could he have imagined in those dark times during rehabilitation that a season that had started in such disappointing fashion would end on a high with him in the Atletico Madrid first team.

Before that, however, came more success in the junior ranks, but this time not in the colours of his club, but in the red-and-gold of his country when he helped Spain win the Algarve Tournament, in which he finished as the top scorer. And a couple of months later came international glory on an even bigger stage, at the 2001 UEFA Under-16 European Championship. Coincidentally, the tournament was held in England and, just as he has since swapping Madrid for Merseyside, Fernando flourished.

Spain topped their qualifying group with two wins from three matches, scoring eight goals and conceding only two, before finally overcoming Italy in a hard-fought quarter-final which ended 1–1 after extra-time, with Spain winning through 4–3 after a penalty shoot-out.

A rather more routine 3–0 defeat of Croatia in the semi-finals set up a final meeting with France at Sunderland's Stadium of Light. A narrow 1–0 victory secured the trophy for Spain, their sixth victory at the tournament, making them the event's most successful ever nation. And it was fitting that the young man who scored the winner in the final, from the penalty spot, was Fernando Torres. It was his sixth goal of the tournament and, in front of 29,100 fans, he proved that he had not only the talent for the big occasion, but also the temperament.

It was an event and an occasion he will never forget and brought him and his team-mates further attention on a wider scale as their success was reported daily on Spanish TV and in the country's newspapers. And at the tender age of just 15 or 16, that recognition is something a player cannot help but be excited about. As the tournament progressed and interest grew still further in their achievements, the young Spanish starlets were all aware that they had a real chance to make names for themselves. Even in those days, however, they recognised that once they reached the final against France they had to win it. After all, people rarely remember the runners-up in finals. But win they did, of course, and the following day they found their exploits reported on the front page of the nation's media.

Fernando was chosen as the player of the tournament, just as he had been at the Nike Cup, and, on his return to Madrid, he noticed a marked change in people's perceptions of him. He was now being recognised in the street and was earmarked as one to watch. And those people highlighting his potential didn't have to wait long for him to start to fulfil it. Just a few weeks after returning from the Under-16 Championship in England, he was told by the club's coaching staff that he would be joining the first-team squad for training for the remainder of the season, in readiness, he believed, to begin the next pre-season with the senior group. He received that information on the Tuesday evening; on Wednesday he underwent his first training session with the first team, and the following Sunday he made his senior debut at Vicente Calderon against Leganes – just three weeks to the day after his goal had won the Under-16 Championship for Spain.

It was a crucial game for Atletico, in front of a packed house on a swelteringly hot day – the tension was palpable. The hosts had to win to keep alive their hopes of promotion from the second division. For the debut boy, though, the sheer excitement of the occasion overpowered any nerves he might be feeling. He was simply dying to play and, in the end, all went well as Atletico clinched a 1-0 victory. For the teenage striker, it was the realisation of a boyhood dream but, even though he had achieved his aims at such a young stage, even then he knew it was not the culmination of his ambitions, merely the beginning.

There was to be no debut goal, but he did not have to wait long to see his name on the score sheet, as just one week later he netted his first for the club against Albacete. There had been much discussion in the week preceding the game as to whether or not Torres would start and, in the end, he was named among the substitutes. He was introduced into the action with 15 minutes remaining, when the score was 0-0. With Atletico again needing to win to maintain their promotion push, he made himself an instant hero when he got under a high ball, positioned himself to shoot ... and fired home his first goal for the first team. Half of the crowd that day were Atleti fans and they went mad, invading the pitch at the end to celebrate an amazing victory.

The season, though, was to end as it had begun, with a rare disappointment as Atletico missed out on promotion to La Liga on goal difference. But, for Fernando, having started the season with a cracked shinbone and ending it as an established member of the first-team squad, with a UEFA Championship tucked away for good measure, it was a season to remember. As he coped with the pain of falling at the last hurdle in the promotion race, though, his previous success was of little comfort to the 17-year-old. He was left to reflect on a season that had promised so much for Atletico but had ultimately delivered so little, as the realisation sunk in that all the hard work the players had put in during the previous months had been for nothing. Everything had looked so good but, in the end, had gone so wrong and the club would have to face another season in the second division. For Torres it meant that the wonderful memories of his debut and his first goal were tainted. They would all have seemed so different had the club's promotion aim been achieved. As it was, however, it now felt like they would have to start again from nothing.

On occasions like that, the dressing room can be a desolate place to be. No one knows how players will react to such disappointment and the Atletico changing room on that day would have been awash with mixed emotions – anger, sadness, devastation, resignation, determination to make amends or, in some cases, acceptance that they had simply fallen short of their target.

It was an early lesson for Torres in the fine margin between success and failure and he has since admitted that, at that stage of his career, the sense of disappointment he felt was more that of a fan than a player. But there was no doubt that the extreme highs and crushing lows of that first month of first team football would stand him n good stead as his career developed.

Fortunately for Torres, he did not have to wait long to taste success in an Atletico jersey, as the following season they achieved their aim of a return to La Liga, two years after being relegated. For the teenage Fernando, however, it was not to be a season of personal triumph. In November, he represented Spain at the 2001 FIFA Under-17 World Championship, a tournament they had qualified for by winning the UEFA Under-16 event the previous May. He scored one goal in three games but, disappointingly, Spain were eliminated at the first group stage, finishing third behind Argentina and Burkina

Faso, both of whom had beaten them. And back at home, although Atletico achieved their promotion goal, Fernando's goal ratio was a poor one, with a return of only six in 36 games. But promotion was all that counted and 18-year-old Fernando could look forward to starting the 2002/03 season in Spain's top division. Still, he felt a sense of personal under-achievement.

He had set high standards for himself despite his tender years and his return of six goals was a disappointment, particularly given the expectations people had of him. Football is a team game, though, and individual glory has to come second to collective success so, with promotion achieved, Torres could look back with pride on a job well done.

Even then, though, there was a slight sense of disappointment that Atletico had been unable to celebrate their triumph in the way they had hoped. They had a chance to do so by beating Nastic in front of their own fans at the Vicente Calderon, but a last-minute equaliser for the visitors robbed them of their moment of glory. Instead, results the following day confirmed their promotion and the players later admitted they would have preferred to wait a week or two to be able to celebrate at their home ground with the fans. Instead, later that evening, they partied alone.

That was not to be the end of the season for Fernando, though. There was still more football to be played and, in July, he travelled with Spain to Norway for the UEFA Under-19 European Championship, the first time the event had been contested at that age group, having been reclassified from an Under-18 event. And it was to be another memorable tournament for Spain and for

Fernando in particular. Two wins and a draw in the group stages meant they went through to the final as group winners, where their opponents would be Germany. Once more, just as in England in the Under-16 event the previous year, Spain won the final 1–0 thanks to a goal from Torres.

And once again he was top scorer and Player of the Tournament. As you would expect, he remembers those triumphs at youth level with great affection. 'I watch matches I played in a long time ago,' he said later in an interview with uefa.com. 'The good ones and the bad. When I've got nothing to do, I watch games from the Under-16 and Under-19 Championships. They bring back memories and give me a little boost.'

And so it was that he prepared for his first season in La Liga, Spain's premier division, in good spirits following a successful summer. But he knew that the pressure and the expectation on him would increase significantly in the top flight.

2

A LEGEND
IS BORN

Fernando Torres has had to live with pressure throughout his entire career. But now, as he approaches his mid-twenties, he understands how to deal with it and has faith and confidence in his own ability. But, as he readied himself for the start of the 2002/03 season, there must have been doubts, however small, in his own mind.

After a below-par goal return during Atletico's second division title-winning season the previous term, the young Fernando knew that people were waiting to see whether or not his undoubted promise would be fulfilled and if he could make the step up to the next level. And he knew that the club's fans were expecting big things from him as Madrid returned to the top flight, their rightful place according to the Vicente Calderon faithful. And there were few in world football who would argue with that. The club are one of the most successful in Spanish league history, having won both La Liga and the Copa del Rey on nine occasions, including that double triumph in 1996. In terms of league title successes, that makes them the third most decorated club in the country, albeit lagging some distance behind Barcelona (18 titles) and city rivals Real Madrid, who lead the way with 31. But, for a much smaller club with far fewer resources, that nonetheless represents a significant success rate and one of which the supporters are rightfully proud.

Famous ex-players include Luis Aragones, who recently coached Spain to glory at Euro 2008, Argentinean star Diego Simeone, former Dutch international striker Jimmy Floyd Hasselbaink, Mexican goalscoring ace Hugo Sanchez and Portuguese legend Paulo Futre. The club have also been coached by luminaries such as Aragones, Cesar Luis Menotti, Ron Atkinson, Arrigo Saachi and Claudio Ranieri.

Atletico also have one of the most distinctive kits in European football, the famous red-and-white striped shirts and blue shorts. However, when the club were founded in 1903, they played in blue-and-white striped shirts, the same as Athletic Bilbao, and there are a number of theories as to why they later changed to red-and-white stripes. The most popular one is that red-and-white shirts were cheaper to make because the stripes were the same as those used to make bed mattresses, and the leftover material could be used to make the football shirts. It was at that time that the club became known as 'Los Colchoneros', the Mattress Makers.

Whatever the reason, it is a kit that is known throughout Europe and its players are proud to sport the famous colours. Torres was no exception and, as he approached his first La Liga season, the feats of the legendary strikers of the past must have been playing on his mind as he set about establishing himself among the elite of Spanish football.

For all young players, their first season at the highest level is a test. Even those who pass with flying colours are constantly being asked new questions and having to come up with new answers. Torres was certainly tested but, as the best always do, he found a way to succeed, and the doubters need not have worried. He scored 13 goals in 29 La Liga games, a more than respectable return for a young striker and one that ensured he finished as the team's top scorer. He performed well throughout the season as Atletico finished comfortably in mid-table and he was particularly impressive in home matches against big guns like Deportivo La Coruña and Barcelona. Those stellar displays brought him to the attention of an ever wider audience in Spain, and earned him his first call-up to the national Under-21 team.

Torres was now becoming an established star and beginning to feature prominently in the media, especially in the football-mad Madrid newspapers. And, as his profile grew, so too did the demands on his time from Atletico fans, eager to be seen with the club's new talisman. Not that the attention bothered him unduly. He was then, and remains so today, an accessible person and believes that signing autographs after training sessions is something that players should always do. Perhaps that sense of duty comes from his recognition that not so long ago he was a wide-eyed kid who felt the same love and affection for his Atletico Madrid heroes as Liverpool's young fans feel for him today, and he takes great pride in his importance to the supporters. And, whether they like it or not, the high profile of

Premier League players today means that, rightly or wrongly, they are viewed almost as 'public property'.

That loss of privacy is the price today's top stars are forced to pay, and it was clear to all that Fernando was well on his way to becoming one of the game's leading lights, not just in Spain, but also across Europe and the world. And if there were any remaining doubts about his talents, those were expelled for good during the 2003/04 season, his second in La Liga. He scored 19 goals in 35 games at a ratio of better than a goal every two games, finishing third top scorer in the league behind Real Madrid's Brazilian superstar Ronaldo and Julio Baptista of Sevilla.

And, at the age of just 19, he was also named as the captain of Atletico Madrid, the youngest player ever to have that honour bestowed on him. It truly was the stuff of dreams for a young man who had harboured such ambitions from an early age.

There was to be disappointment at the end of the season, though, as Atletico Madrid slipped to a finishing spot of seventh, missing out on European football and a place in the following season's UEFA Cup. It was a bitter pill for Fernando to swallow, particularly as the side had been in the European qualification spots for much of the campaign.

There was the consolation of a place in the Intertoto Cup, with the prize for the winners being a UEFA Cup berth. It meant, of course, a short close season for Fernando and his team-mates, but there would be no complaints if European football was secured at the end of it.

Atletico battled through to the final, only to lose 3–1 on penalties to La Liga rivals Villarreal, following a 2–2 aggregate draw. It was another devastating blow for Fernando to endure. He was desperate to win a trophy with his home-town club but, just as it's hard for Premier League clubs in England to compete on a level playing field with the 'Big Four' of Arsenal, Chelsea, Liverpool and Manchester United, so too Real Madrid and Barcelona dominate Spanish football. And, clearly, when you are playing for Atletico, for long periods of time you have to cope with living in the shadows of the men in white who play at the Bernabeu.

The following season, 2004/05, brought no success either. In fact, the team did not perform as well in La Liga, slumping to a disappointing 11th place finish, although Fernando again finished as top scorer with 16 goals. They did perform better in the Copa del Rey, but ultimately that campaign ended in frustration as well, with the team from Madrid losing over two legs to Osasuna in the semi-finals. Fernando confessed after that defeat to being 'bitterly disappointed' as his hopes of finally landing a trophy faded once more.

But the young striker's impact in La Liga was beginning to be noticed more and more by overseas suitors, with Premier League clubs in England particularly interested in the striker they called 'El Niño', The Kid, a reference to his boyish good looks. Big-spending Chelsea, with Roman Abramovich's billions to play with, were among the first to declare an interest in him in the summer of 2005. However, it was interest that was swiftly and unceremoniously rejected by Atletico officials. While confirming that a meeting had taken place between Chelsea's Chief Executive, Peter Kenyon, and Atletico's major shareholder, Miguel Angel Gil, on 19 June, club president Enrique Cerezo was unequivocal in his message to the wealthy Russian. He told Spanish sports paper *Marca*, 'Abramovich should forget about signing Torres. He is an Atletico player and will be for many years.'

With that raid on their star striker successfully repelled, Atletico made a mixed start to the 2005/06 season, winning only one of their first five La Liga games. Bizarrely, their solitary success came in almost certainly their toughest challenge in those early stages of the campaign, at home to Barcelona. Their task in that match was made tougher still when they fell behind after only six minutes to a goal from Barça's Cameroon international striker Samuel Eto'o. Torres, though, restored parity in the 17th minute and Atletico went on to win the game 2–1 thanks to a winning goal from former Chelsea striker Mateja Kezman two minutes into the second half.

Inexplicably, though, they followed that fantastic win with an away defeat at Real Sociedad and a home loss to little Getafe. That was the sort of inconsistency that would plague them throughout the season which had started with such high hopes under a new coach, Argentinean Carlos Bianchi, a man who had enjoyed considerable success in South America with Selez Varsfield and Boca Juniors, including winning four Copa Libertadores, with Selez in 1994 and with Boca in 2000, 2001 and 2003. Despite his pedigree, however, he failed to inspire Atletico and left midway through the season, just as he had on his previous foray into European football, with Italians Roma in 1996. He was succeeded by José Murcia, who was coach to the club's B team, and he succeeded in stopping the rot, including overseeing a run of six successive victories early in the New Year that inspired thoughts of a late run into the European qualification spots.

But while there were considerable highs, notably those six wins on the bounce and a 3–1 victory over Barcelona in the Nou Camp, with Torres claiming the first and third goals to complete a memorable league double over the Catalan giants, there were also several lows, not least of which was a run of four home defeats in five games in the closing stages of the season to Sevilla, Celta Vigo, Mallorca and Osasuna. Those sorts of results, coupled with far too many draws, conspired to condemn Atletico to tenth place in the table, 12 points adrift of the UEFA Cup places and a full 30 points behind eventual champions Barcelona, a team they had beaten twice.

It was another below-par season for the team and another low point for Torres, although once again, his goal return was healthy – 13 goals in 36 La Liga matches – meaning he was once more the club's leading scorer. That was of little consolation to him, though, as he contemplated another season of under-achievement by the club as a whole. In truth, although the players believed the club had recruited a good coach in Bianchi, he had not gelled with the team and, likewise, they had not bedded in well with him, making for a very difficult first part of the season in La Liga. And although the appointment of Murcia calmed the troubled waters and gave the squad fresh belief, they had left themselves too much ground to make up to claim a place in Europe.

But, while admitting that the club's form had been inconsistent, Torres had again proved his own consistency, scoring double figures in La Liga for the fourth season running. And Europe's vultures were now beginning to circle with ever-increasing purpose, with Barcelona, AC Milan and Arsenal all reportedly interested in signing the striker.

Interestingly, it appeared Atletico's resolve to keep him was beginning to wane. Cerezo admitted in January 2006, 'I'm obliged to listen to offers for Torres just like any other player. You study the offer and see what happens. But we're not a club that sells and we have no intention of selling Torres for the sake of it.'

And, in March that year, Fernando himself admitted that Newcastle had made a bid to sign him. He told the *Sun* newspaper, 'There has always been talk about lots of clubs but I only know of one firm offer and that's from Newcastle. I've never thought about listening to offers from anyone but you can never be certain about what may happen.'

With reported interest also coming from Tottenham, and with Arsenal and Chelsea known admirers, it was beginning to look as though England would be a likely destination for him at the end of the season. After all, Fernando had confessed an interest in a move to Arsenal the previous November, saying, 'If Arsenal, and a coach like Arsène Wenger want to speak to you, it's really flattering. They are in the Champions League every season and I want to play against the best and challenge for the biggest titles.'

But before the outcome of where he may or not begin the 2006/07 domestic season could be resolved, there was the small matter of a World Cup finals in Germany to prepare for, as Spain, who once again would begin the event among the favourites to lift the trophy, set about trying to rid themselves of the unwanted tag of perennial under-achievers. It was a label that many Spanish national sides had had to live with down the years since their one and only international triumph at the 1964 European

Championship. Could this be the year when they finally delivered on all that promise?

A star at junior level, having won major honours in Under-16 and Under-19 tournaments, Torres was one of the players on whom Spain's hopes rested and he had been earmarked for great things for a number of years. Having served his apprenticeship in the junior ranks and at Under-21 level, Fernando received his first call-up for the senior squad for their friendly against Portugal in September 2003, still aged only 19. And, as anyone will tell you, only the most special of talents are thrust into the international spotlight before they are out of their teens.

Torres admits to feeling the nerves in the build-up to the match but, typically, once his ascension to the full squad was confirmed, he took it in his stride, just as he had done with all the challenges he had faced in his career to date. There had been much speculation that he would be involved, but he later confessed that he didn't think it would happen. But, of course, it was only a matter of time before he added senior international honours to those he had won at age group levels. Imagine the excitement, however, of the youngster meeting up for the first time with players he had grown up watching on television and the feelings of awe he must have had. Most young players called up for international duty for the first time will talk of the nerves they felt entering an environment in which everybody knows each other and is comfortable in their surroundings. For Torres, those fears and uncertainties would have been as real as for any of those players that had gone before him, but the established stars welcomed him into the fold.

If he felt apprehensive off the pitch around Spain's senior stars, he suffered no such inferiority complex on the training ground or on the pitch. And so it was that he was handed his debut. It proved to be a comfortable night for Spain as they ran out 3–0 winners, but less comfortable for the teenage debutant who found himself forced off injured before half-time. It was a disappointing end to one of the biggest nights of his life, but Fernando was in philosophical mood afterwards, admitting, 'I was really up for the game and, even though the Portuguese defenders forced me out of it, I came off the pitch happy because now I've made my debut and that will live with me for ever.'

Torres remained a fixture in the squad as the side continued their preparation for Euro 2004 in Portugal. And, just a couple of months before the start of that tournament, he netted his first goal for his country, a strike that surely cemented his place in the final squad for what would be his first major championship at senior level.

That goal came against Italy at the end of April 2004, thanks, in part, to a lucky omen. For the first time in his senior international career he had been allowed to wear the number 14 shirt, the shirt he had worn at junior levels where he had enjoyed so much success. So it was no surprise to him that he opened his account for his country that night, although he did admit after the match that he was not totally satisfied with his night's work against the Italians and felt an annoyance that, even though he had scored his first goal, he felt he could have had more.

No striker is ever truly happy with his performance unless he leaves the pitch with a goal to his credit at the end of 90 minutes. Fernando, it appears, is not satisfied even with that. Despite being his own harshest critic he was, as predicted, named in the final squad for Portugal and naturally he approached the tournament with a great deal of youthful exuberance. The European Championship had been at the forefront of his thoughts and he had been determined to have a good season on the pitch to make sure he was in the squad. In his favour, of course, was the fact that the coach, Inaki Saez, knew all about his attributes from their time together in the junior ranks. Once his place was confirmed, Torres could then turn his attention to trying to force his way into the starting line-up ahead of Spain's more established striking stars, convinced that he was now ready to prove his worth on the biggest stage.

In fact, there was to be no place in the starting line-up for Fernando for Spain's first group game against Russia, with coach Saez preferring the experience of Fernando Morientes and Raul up front. Torres had to be content with a 12-minute cameo from the bench as a late replacement for Raul.

But, although he certainly didn't get as much time on the pitch as he would have liked, the key thing for Fernando and his team-mates was that they got the three points they desperately wanted from their opening fixture. That meant they approached their second, and possibly crucial match against Greece, in good spirits. The Greeks had stunned the host nation in their opening game by recording a highly unexpected 2-1 win, meaning that the victors of the Spain–Greece clash would book themselves a place in the last eight with a game to spare.

However, neither side was able to force a win, and they settled for a point apiece in a 1-1 draw. With Portugal battling back from their opening-night nerves to beat Russia, it meant Spain went into their final group game, against the hosts, knowing that avoiding defeat would be enough to send them through to the quarter-finals.

Torres had once again appeared as a late substitute for Raul in the draw against Greece, but, for the decisive game against Portugal, coach Saez decided that the Atletico Madrid youngster would start in attack alongside the Real Madrid captain, with Morientes the man to make way. It was a decision that, sadly for the Spanish, did not pay off. Torres had a couple of half-decent chances, but could not find a way past Portuguese goalkeeper Ricardo, nor could any of his team-mates. And their failures in front of goal meant it was Portugal who progressed to the knockout stages at the expense of their Iberian rivals, courtesy of a winning goal from substitute Nuno Gomes 12 minutes into the second half.

It was a bitter blow for the Spaniards who, after their opening victory against the Russians, had failed to take advantage of that promising start. Saez admitted, 'The players are extremely low. We had great hopes for this tournament and had qualification within our grasp, but it wasn't to be. We worked very hard in the first half but they provided all the passion. The goal came from a half-chance and we had to go for the game after that. We had some good chances but the ball just would not go in.'

Goalkeeper Iker Casillas, meanwhile, was damning of his side's performance. He insisted, 'Portugal were all over us. It was our worst game in Euro 2004 and we just didn't give what we had to give. We're going home because we deserve to and that's uncomfortable for all of us. We can't complain about this result.'

Once more, the Spanish had failed to live up to the weight of a nation's expectations, and the country's media was savage in its assessment of the team's performance in Portugal. The influential *Marca* proclaimed, 'At least our early exit prevents us deluding ourselves. We can blame Saez but the problem is much more complex. Our lack of mental strength, lack of action and the weight of history proves too big a burden for each new generation of Spanish soccer players.'

The *AS* sports daily was similarly harsh on the under-performing squad, saying, 'Spain failed again and this time without an ounce of glory or even dignity. There is nothing good to take from this tournament. They didn't play well, they can't blame a difficult draw or the referee, and there were no heroes.'

La Razon newspaper, meanwhile, laid the blame firmly at the feet of Saez, claiming he had picked 'his favourite players' rather than those 'in better physical and mental shape'.

With so much flak flying, it was little surprise when Saez announced his resignation following Spain's early exit. He said, 'I have given the reasons for taking a decision which I will not go back on, which is to stop training the national side.'

For Torres, the tournament proved to be a bittersweet experience. Although not a member of the first choice XI, that did not get him down. Instead, he revelled in the experience, likening it to being with the Under-16s or the Under-19s, but even better to be in a finals with the national team at the highest level you can aim for.

He was at the top of the international game and was rightly savouring it. What did not occur to Torres, nor to his team-mates, was that after winning their first game and drawing their second with Greece, they would fail to make the quarter-finals such was the confidence with which they approached the game against Portugal. The feeling of desolation once they were knocked out enveloped the squad and Torres later admitted that he did not know how they failed to beat the hosts.

That defeat was a disastrous result for Spain and the players could only watch helplessly as the Portuguese players and supporters enjoyed their moment of glory, suffering alone and having to witness the disappointment in the eyes of their own fans and team-mates. It was a setback that was desperately hard to take and it took Torres several days to really take in the fact they had been knocked out.

But out they were and the task of new coach Luis Aragones was to restore the squad's morale as they set about the task of qualifying for the 2006 World Cup finals in Germany. On paper, Spain's qualifying group did not look the toughest proposition. They found themselves in Group Seven along with Bosnia-Herzegovina, Belgium, Lithuania, San Marino and Serbia & Montenegro. It was a group they were hotly tipped to win.

They survived their ten matches unbeaten, but five wins and five draws were not enough for them to top the group and they finished second behind Serbia & Montenegro, meaning they missed out on automatic qualification. Instead, they would have to overcome one further hurdle; a two-legged play-off against Slovakia. It was a challenge they overcame with ease, winning the first leg 5–1 and rendering the second meeting, which ended 1–1, all but meaningless.

The qualification campaign had been a success for Torres as he scored seven of Spain's 19 goals to make him the fourth top scorer in the European qualification section. And it was with that strike rate behind him that he approached the tournament as one of the players tipped to make a real impact, and Europe's leading clubs remained on red alert as they planned their post-World Cup spending sprees.

It was a stage on which he could not wait to perform. After their disappointment at Euro 2004, the players were determined to make amends and reaching the finals in Germany was almost an obligation, not merely an ambition. There was a sense among the squad that they had a collective need to exorcise the ghosts of Portugal and there was a steely determination that they should not fall short of their goal. That desire could be seen on the faces of the players as they lined up for the national anthems before games and it was one shared by the supporters, starved for so long of genuine success.

But all of the players were aware that they had made hard work of the qualifying campaign and would have to improve significantly if they were to emerge as real contenders for the biggest prize in football. Torres knew, too, that he had work to do. Even though he finished the qualifying campaign as his country's top scorer, enhancing his growing reputation in the process, he was well aware that the finals themselves represented another step up in class. But it was a test he felt ready for. Indeed, it was one he had been preparing for all his adult life and, if truth be told, through most of his childhood years as well.

The World Cup had been something he had fantasised about on summer nights as a boy as he kicked a ball around and, as he arrived in Germany, his sense of excitement became even more heightened.

'I had been fighting all my life for a dream, to play with the best in the world, and finally I had it within reach. I was going to play in the World Cup!' he later said on his website. 'When I got there, everything around me smelled of football, but what really surprised me was seeing so many people wearing red shirts who had come from Spain to support us. Not even in Portugal during Euro 2004 did I see so many of our fans. And they all thought this could be Spain's year for the World Cup. We had players of a high quality, and overall we formed a solid and young team. We had high aims.'

The tournament could not have begun in better fashion for Spain, who opened their Group H account with a crushing 4–0 win over Ukraine, the team expected to provide the sternest test to them during the first phase. Xabi Alonso and David Villa (2) gave the Spaniards a commanding 3–0 lead before Torres finished off the scoring in the 81st minute, providing the final touch to a sweeping Spanish move when he drilled the ball home. It was the perfect start for the side ranked fifth in the world and, with games against Tunisia and Saudi Arabia to come, qualification for the second round was surely a formality. Coach Aragones admitted, 'If we show what we can do, I know we can be among the top teams at this tournament. At first, I thought it was going to be more complicated but the second goal made Ukraine more crestfallen and the rest was easier.

'We didn't expect such a good start, but we were lucky to score early goals from two set-pieces and that gave us the calmness we needed and created more space so that we could control the game. We need to make a fair analysis of the game. We enjoyed all the luck and it's very difficult to win 4–0 in a World Cup, but what is clear is that the players knew exactly what they had to do.

'Historically, we have done nothing even though we have attended World Cups for the last 30 years. This time we hope to do something, but we've got a very difficult game in five days against Tunisia. We have to take each game at a time and Tunisia are a better footballing side than Ukraine. We've got great respect for all our rivals and that goes for Tunisia as well.'

But, for all Aragones' words of warning about not taking the challenge from the north Africans lightly, he must surely have fully expected his side to brush them aside. And they did just that, although they did have to recover from the shock of conceding an 8th-minute goal, but, whereas previous Spanish sides may have panicked at that early setback, the class of 2006 eased themselves back into the match and finally ran out comfortable 3–1 winners.

The goals came from Raul and Torres, who scored twice, the second a penalty. So, with three goals from his two games, the Atletico Madrid hot-shot was now the tournament's top scorer. All was well in the world.

Aragones, though, was a relieved man at the end of the match. He reflected, 'I knew it would be a very complicated and difficult game. They caught us on the break in the first half and then shut up at the back and it was tremendously difficult for us to break through.'

Torres also had words of praise for Spain's opponents and insisted that Tunisia had provided a stern test for him and his team-mates. He told the media after the game, 'It was harder than we expected but it is important to win any way you can. The team showed spirit and did not get downhearted when they were behind.'

As for his own goalscoring exploits, he was too polite to promote his own individual cause, instead insisting, 'As long as the strikers keep scoring, we will progress in this tournament.'

And progress they did, through to the knockout stages after making it three wins out of three in their qualifying group. With their safe passage already secured, Aragones changed his entire first XI, meaning Fernando sat out his first game of the tournament, although he did enjoy a brief 20-minute run-out off the bench for the closing stages.

Even with their second-string team in action, Spain proved too strong for the Saudis, claiming a third successive win, this time by a score of 1–0. For Aragones, it was job done but he knew that his team had been in a battle. He said, 'We didn't play too badly in the first half and maybe could have had another goal, but fell apart in the second and were at their mercy. They deserved to score a goal and get at least a draw from the match.'

But the win mattered far more than the performance and it booked the Spanish a last-16 meeting with France, a game that would provide a far stiffer test of their resolve and their abilities to really make a mark on the tournament. And it was a test the players were ready for. Liverpool midfielder Xabi Alonso, while insisting his side were taking nothing for granted after their unbeaten start to the tournament, admitted, 'The atmosphere is always better when you are performing well and winning games. But we know it's a tough competition so we have to focus and concentrate. We want to go as far as possible.

'It was a boost winning the first two games because that meant we reached the knockout stage. That's what we wanted. Now we have rested some players and, at the same time, confidence in the team is high. But now we want to continue and show it on the pitch.'

One man whose confidence was certainly high was Torres, particularly as he was being linked with a £20m move to Manchester United on the back of his goalscoring exploits in Spain's first two games. And his team-mates were hoping he would continue his hot streak against the French.

Arsenal midfield star Cesc Fabregas told reporters on the eve of the match, 'Torres is a very quick player. He's very competitive. He's a winner and you always like to have this kind of player in your team.' He added, 'We are playing well at the moment. The confidence is very high in the team and country, and I think we just have to keep going with the same mentality. We will try to go as far as we can but it is very difficult as there are a lot of very big teams. We are a very young team and we are working very hard. Everyone wants to be in the first XI so I think that is very important for the competition in the team. It is very difficult to get to the final but all I'm sure of is that we have a great team and a great manager. I'm sure we have all the right conditions to win the World Cup.'

Unfortunately for Spain, however, they suffered familiar pain as they once more failed their big test, crashing out 3–1 to the French as a tournament that had started so promisingly ended again in bitter failure. Coach Aragones, however, was unhappy about the award of the free-kick that led to France's second goal and ultimately turned the game very much in their favour. He complained, 'It came from a free-kick that wasn't a foul and we were punished by a refereeing error. When players give everything, you can't ask any more. They're still young and have another chance in the future. Football is unjust sometimes, but not always. France were very tough opponents.'

And once again, just as it had been two years earlier, it was left to keeper Casillas to sum up the mood in the Spanish camp. He said, 'We were so close. It was undeserved, an undeserved defeat. But that's football, we're heading home and there's nothing we can do about it.'

Spain's players returned to their native country to begin preparations for the new La Liga season, but Fernando's future was still up in the air with continued speculation that he might leave Madrid. In fact, perhaps surprisingly given his performances in Germany, he stayed with the La Liga side, although he later revealed that he could have moved to England – and Chelsea. He said, 'It was possible to join Chelsea [after the World Cup], but I decided to be ruled by my heart. I wanted to have success with Atletico Madrid.'

Chelsea were not the only team keen to sign Spain's new golden boy and he admitted that he could have taken one of several offers to move. Instead, however, he chose to show his commitment to the club of his dreams by signing an extension to his contract which would keep him at the Vicente Calderon Stadium until 2009.

So it was a contented and settled Fernando Torres who began the

2006/07 season, desperate to bring some success to Atletico in terms of silverware or, at the very least, a place in Europe for the following campaign.

Once more, however, they made an inconsistent start to the season, with good victories against Athletic Bilbao and Sevilla, and an excellent 1–1 draw at the Bernabeu in the Madrid derby, being undermined by disappointing home defeats to Valencia and Real Zaragoza.

Following that loss to Zaragoza, though, they embarked on a run of 12 games in which they suffered only one defeat in three months, terrific form by anyone's standards and they were firmly in among the challengers for those European places. Indeed, at the end of January, they were in fifth place in the La Liga table, just four points behind the leaders Barcelona. And, by the end of February, they were still fifth and very much in the hunt for Champions League qualification. Indeed, as they approached the return meeting with Real Madrid at Vicente Calderon, they knew that a win would take them level on points with their great city rivals.

And, in fact, victory in that match would mean they would go above Real on the head-to-head rule courtesy of their 1–1 draw at the Bernabeu earlier in the season. But, having lost to other top-of-the-table rivals Valencia and Sevilla in the weeks building up to the big derby, they were keen to make certain there were no mistakes this time.

Coach Javier Aguirre told a news conference on the eve of the match, 'We haven't performed against two other direct rivals of late and this is a third chance we cannot let slip by. Our results haven't been too good in the last few weeks and we are keen to prove our worth again.'

The game could scarcely have started any better for Atletico as Torres opened the scoring after just 11 minutes. It was a lead the home side held until midway through the second half when they were finally undone by Gonzalo Higuain's equaliser, meaning the sides had to settle for a second draw between them that season.

Although a point meant Atletico remained outside the Champions League places, it was far from a disaster. But what followed – with four defeats in their next nine La Liga matches – certainly took its toll on their hopes of earning a place in Europe's premier club competition.

But as they approached their final big test of the season, a home game against joint leaders Barcelona, who now shared top spot with Real Madrid, they were still very much in the shake-up for an automatic European place, albeit in the UEFA Cup, as they went into the game lying in sixth place. And they could approach the contest with justifiable confidence, having not lost in their previous five games against the Catalan giants. And in Torres, who had scored six goals in those five games, they had a weapon that Barça were clearly extremely wary of.

Midfielder Andres Iniesta admitted, 'It's true we haven't enjoyed much luck in the Vicente Calderon in recent games, but circumstances change and, now that we need a win, maybe things will change. Atletico base much of their play around Torres' pace, and when he is given a lot of space he can be very dangerous. We have to be alert to stop these balls getting through to him.'

Atletico coach Aguirre, meanwhile, was expecting a tense tussle but one his team were capable of winning. He told reporters at his pre-match press conference, 'Both teams have everything still to play for, and we will both know everyone else's results when we take to the pitch. Everyone talks about Barça's recent poor results but I think their performances have been good. They are joint leaders and we shouldn't underestimate them. It's a good chance for us to make our mark on the season, put on a performance for the fans, and prove that we are a team worthy of a place in Europe next season.'

Sadly for Aguirre, for Torres and for all the Atletico players and fans, they failed woefully in that task of proving they deserved a European place for the first time in six years as they slumped to an embarrassing 6–0 home defeat. Atletico's players left the pitch that night to a chorus of whistles and boos, and Fernando would later admit that humiliation was the catalyst for his eventual decision to quit Madrid. He told *FourFourTwo* magazine, 'That was a key day, for sure, maybe the day that I was finally convinced to leave... after losing 6–0 and seeing the way it happened, after seeing all the fans, who had always been right behind their team but now weren't, after seeing the sense of tiredness and fatigue about it all. The fans didn't deserve that and a team that's used to winning just doesn't go through an experience like that.

'I was really hurt. For me, for the fans, for the team. When I saw the Barcelona players leaving having won 6–0, I felt jealous of them, jealous of the fact that they played for a big club that always aspires to the biggest successes, that's capable of going to the Calderon and winning 6–0.'

Fernando did confess, however, that he felt some Atletico

supporters were happy to see their side lose to Barcelona if it meant the Catalans winning La Liga instead of Real Madrid. He continued, 'At all clubs, the fans really hate their rivals and keep an eye on their results but one of the problems we always had at Atletico was that the fans were too focused on Real Madrid; that was symbolic of our bad times. When you're not achieving anything, you focus on your rivals and hope they lose. But you reach the point where you think it's time we looked at ourselves, thought about our own results and left Real Madrid alone. If your fans want you to lose, it's a sign that your team has nothing to play for. And when that dawns on you, it hurts.'

That defeat, while damaging, wasn't the end of the world for Atletico and, with three games remaining in the La Liga season, they were clinging on to sixth place and that final UEFA Cup spot with their destiny still in their own hands. And, after the demoralising nature of that Barcelona defeat, they had the perfect chance to restore their fragile confidence when they visited rock-bottom Gimnastic for their next fixture the following week.

Captain Torres was in defiant mood as he faced the media in the pre-match press conference. He said, 'The team did not perform to the standards expected [last weekend] and Barcelona were much better. We didn't have the correct attitude. It was one of those days where it would have been better to have stayed in bed. We have to forget about it quickly and focus on 'Nastic. It was a one-off and we can't wallow in self-pity. We need to recall the attitude we had against Getafe in the match before we played Barcelona [where they won 4–1].'

And Fernando pleaded for patience after a difficult week for the club in the wake of that Barça debacle, with fans and the media speculating on the futures of several players, as well as of coach Aguirre and sporting director Jesus Garcia Pitarch.

The talismanic striker added, 'Since we were relegated in 2000, these have been some of the worst years for the club, but we still hold this dream of returning to being among the top six. Ever since I have been in the first team, we have had big changes every season with a new coach, and changes among the players. This year we are so close to achieving our objective of a place in the UEFA Cup. We have to have confidence in the project and only make changes that will help to improve the situation. We only need minor changes in my opinion. We need to look at the success of teams like Villarreal and Sevilla who have had long-term plans, continuity and stood by their coaches.'

On the pitch, Torres backed up the words he had delivered so passionately off it by scoring both goals as Atletico ran out 2-0 winners to remain on course for Europe. With two games to go, they knew that two wins would see them achieve their Holy Grail.

But those hopes suffered a setback in the build-up to the penultimate game against Celta Vigo when Torres suffered an ankle injury in training that forced him to pull out of Spain's squad for the Euro 2008 qualifiers against Latvia and Liechtenstein. But, as the crucial league fixture approached, Fernando became more and more resolute in his desire to play in such a vital encounter and Aguirre was hopeful that his leading scorer would be fit to lead the line. He said, 'Torres is much better. He is very enthusiastic, is very strong mentally and I don't think a twisted ankle is going to deny him this opportunity.

After having played four years with the club outside Europe, he wants to make sure he participates.'

Torres underwent a late fitness test and was given the all-clear to play, but sadly his presence still was not enough to prevent Atletico from slipping to a shock defeat against another of La Liga's strugglers. Celta Vigo could have been relegated at the Vicente Calderon had they lost and other results gone against them. Instead, it was Atletico who ended the game in despair as, despite two goals from Argentinean forward Maxi Rodriguez, they crashed to a disastrous 3–2 defeat. And little did anyone realise at the time it would be Fernando's final appearance at the ground he had been so proud to call home for so long.

That result meant they approached the final game of the campaign with European qualification no longer in their own hands, having slipped out of the top six for the first time in ten months. They needed to win at Osasuna while hoping that the results in the games of the sides in fifth and sixth place, Real Zaragoza and Villarreal, went in their favour and rescued their season.

And, as you would expect, it was a naturally tense Aguirre who faced the media ahead of the Osasuna clash. He said, 'We are playing the whole season in these 90 minutes. Unfortunately our destiny is out of our hands now because we have let slip various opportunities to be in control of the situation. But we still have a legitimate chance to make it into Europe. We have to give our all to get the three points in Pamplona, and then hope things go our way elsewhere. Over the course of the season, we have proven we have committed, quality players and that we deserve to be in Europe.'

The Mexican coach was well aware that his position at the club was under threat, despite the public backing of Torres and other senior players, but he insisted that his focus was only on the job in hand, adding, 'I signed a one-year contract last summer and, on Monday, when we know where we stand, we can sit down and talk again. The team comes first.'

Atletico did their job, just, securing a somewhat fortuitous 2–1 win thanks to an own-goal from Osasuna defender Nacho Monreal, but it proved to be irrelevant as Zaragoza's draw against Recreativo ensured they grabbed the final European place by virtue of their better head-to-head record against Atletico.

Fernando later revealed on his personal website, 'Events on the pitch at Atletico were no better than last year. On the final day of the season, we missed out on a place in Europe, a position we had defended since September. Once again, I went off on holiday feeling that we had not achieved our objectives. All the hard work we had put in disappeared in the blink of an eye.'

It was clear from those words that Torres was now seriously considering his future at the club. And, although Atletico did eventually qualify for the UEFA Cup, via the Intertoto Cup, thus securing European football for the first time in seven years, the man who had worked so hard to achieve that dream would not be there to share the adventure.

3

A NEW BEGINNING

With Torres now seemingly disenchanted with life at Atletico and growing frustrated at the club's lack of success, it was inevitable that it would lead to a parting of the ways. No matter how much affection a player has for his home-town club, it is very rare these days that he will settle long term for what would appear to be 'second best', and even rarer still in the case of a top star like Fernando Torres.

Speculation was rife as to where he would move, but it did appear that England was the most likely destination with the 'Big Four' of Arsenal, Chelsea, Liverpool and Manchester United all linked with him. Now it was simply a matter of where and when.

It soon became apparent that Liverpool were beginning to edge ahead of their rivals in the transfer hunt, having seemingly decided to make the acquisition of the Spanish star their number-one aim for the summer. Their cause had in fact been aided a month or so previously when a picture of Torres appeared that bizarrely seemed to show he already wore Liverpool's hearts on his sleeve. His captain's armband had slipped during an Atletico Madrid match and on the reverse of it was the inscription 'We'll Never Walk Alone', a slight variation on the Kop's famous anthem.

If it was a subtle hint to Rafael Benitez and the Liverpool money men, it appeared to have done the trick. He later admitted in an interview with liverpoolfc.tv, 'There is a group of my mates, about five or six of us, and we've all grown up supporting Liverpool. Because they are all so committed to Liverpool, they've had "We'll Never Walk Alone" tattooed on their arms. It's changed slightly [from "You'll Never Walk Alone"] because it's a symbol of our friendship as well as our support for the club. Obviously I couldn't have that tattooed on my arm playing for Atletico, but they gave me the armband as a present for my last birthday.'

It takes two parties to make a deal, however, and once more Atletico officials were keen to stress that there had been no official moves for Fernando and that they fully expected him to remain in Spain at the Vicente Calderon. 'We've received no offer from Liverpool or any other club,' insisted Atletico president Enrique Cerezo early that summer. 'There is nothing linking Torres with any team. He's on holiday, he's resting and he will return to work on 9 July. We are now working to create a good team for the coming year.'

But Cerezo did offer some hope to Liverpool, or any other suitor for that matter, when he admitted, 'All the players have a [buy-out] clause in their contract and, in that case, we would not be able to do anything about it.'

So, by his own admission, the door was open for Liverpool to go and get their man, providing they met the Spanish club's valuation of the then 23-year-old. And the Reds wasted no time in making it clear they would be prepared to do just that to land their number-one transfer target.

One ex-Anfield star was convinced the club were getting the right man for the job. Robbie Fowler insisted, 'His goals record has been fantastic in Spain. He has scored plenty of goals for his country as well. I think he will be a great player for Liverpool. I am a Liverpool fan and I hope he brings the championship to the club. Since I have been playing, they've never won that and, as I said before, I am a fan, so I want Liverpool to win everything. Signing players of this calibre will only help the club to get in a position where they can challenge for titles.'

By now it was becoming clear that a deal was imminent and, on 4 July, it was announced that Fernando Torres had signed at Anfield for a club record transfer fee, believed to be around £26.5m.

It was a signing that delighted manager Benitez, who said, 'I am really pleased to have signed Fernando. We know we are bringing a really good young player to Liverpool with a great future ahead of him. We know he is an expensive signing but it's not as much as people have said, and this is a very good investment for us. He is the player we wanted and the kind of player we need because he plays with passion. He has power and pace. He is good in the air and he can score goals. He is a different type of striker to the ones we already have and he can give us a lot of things. He is a very good player who can score a lot of goals for us. I am not going to put pressure on him and say Fernando is going to score over 20 goals in a season for us, because I prefer to have four strikers with 15 goals each.

'Even though he is a young player, he has experience because he was playing in the Spanish First Division when he was just 17. He is desperate to win trophies with us and he wants to win everything that is possible.'

Fernando himself was equally thrilled with the move. He said, 'When the Liverpool offer arrived, I told the club [Atletico] to listen to that offer because that was the team I wanted to play for. It's one of the best, if not the best club, in Europe. It has been a difficult decision to leave my all-time club, but it would have been hard for me to reject Liverpool's offer. It is a big leap for me and I think it was the right time for everyone. The time comes in the life of a player when he needs more challenges.'

Torres was handed the club's famous number 9 shirt when he signed, a shirt that had been worn with distinction by legendary names such as Ian Rush and Robbie Fowler, and he admitted he was thrilled to be bracketed in that sort of company. 'The fact that Liverpool are giving me the number 9 jersey just goes to show the confidence they have placed in me, considering those that have worn that shirt before me. A beautiful new adventure is beginning for me and I hope that with work and effort I can be among the best players.

'This is a unique opportunity for me. Liverpool aspire to win everything and that has been an important factor in my decision to go there. I want to adapt as quickly as possible. I think the Premier League is suited to my style.'

Former Atletico Madrid coach Radomir Antic, who was in charge of the club when Torres first joined them as a boy, agreed with the player's assessment and backed him to be a huge success in England. He told the BBC, 'Liverpool have done a very good job in getting him because Torres is such a good player. I'm surprised Atletico have sold their captain because since he started to play for them he's been important for the team.'

And Antic – who played in England for Luton and famously scored the winning goal against Manchester City in 1983 to keep them in the old First Division, prompting the now famous David Pleat jig across the pitch – also backed Fernando to cope with the physical pressures of the Premier League. Although the fresh-faced Spaniard might have looked like easy pickings for the league's tough guys, Antic insisted he was more than capable of defying any bully-boy tactics, adding, 'England is a good place for his qualities. He has a strong personality, but he's also quick and strong physically. He's also a very skilful player, especially in one-on-one situations, which will be something different for Liverpool up front. They have not had a striker [for a while] who can take the ball and beat opponents. In the last few years at Atletico, he was a striker without any support from midfield. Atletico played that way because his movement meant he could run on to forward passes. He needs a new challenge to improve his game and I think he has made a good move by going to England.'

And it was a challenge Torres was clearly relishing. In his first major interview in English football, he told the Liverpool club website, 'I am very, very happy. This was the biggest decision of my footballing life but I've come to a winning club. This is a club of champions – one of the biggest there is. I now want to play my part in that and be a champion too and help the club progress.

'Obviously, growing up in Spain you are aware of all the big clubs there, but you also keep an eye on Europe, and Liverpool always catches the eye. It always did for me. I had an older brother who'd tell me about the likes of Keegan and Rush, but the first players I remember seeing as a fan are players like Robbie Fowler. My main memory is seeing Liverpool's incredible record in Europe, and I certainly followed that closely.'

And Torres admitted that, as soon as he heard of Liverpool's desire to sign him, his heart was set on a move to Anfield. He continued, 'It was just a couple of weeks ago, it's all happened very quickly. I was aware of offers from other clubs but, as soon as I knew Liverpool were interested, I said to Atletico, "Look, please listen to this offer." There were many clubs being bandied around. Offers go directly to Atletico, so I wouldn't necessarily know about them, but, as soon as I heard about Liverpool, I told them that Anfield was the only place I was interested in.

'I'm aware of the history and how special this club is. The tragedies that have happened have made the bond between the fans and the club so strong. Liverpool just tick all the boxes for me. There's team spirit and a desire to win instilled by Rafa, and then there's my new team-mates like Pepe Reina and Xabi Alonso. They have always spoken very positively about life here in Liverpool. I didn't speak to them directly before signing because it all happened so quickly. I've been getting planes here, there and everywhere.'

And, despite the obvious wrench of leaving the boyhood club of his dreams, the one he has supported all his life, he was convinced he had made the right decision, saying, 'You have certain chances in life. You can't afford to miss them because they only come around once. I've been with Atletico since I was ten... I've grown up as a person and a player there. But we haven't been getting the opportunities to play in Europe and I think I now need to take that step up.'

It was clear that Fernando viewed his move to Anfield as exactly that – a step up – and it was equally clear that he was determined to ensure the move was a success, both for him as a player and for Liverpool as a club. 'If I had the idea I'd already be a success just by joining Liverpool, I wouldn't have come,' he told the *Liverpool Post* newspaper. 'To achieve the level the people here demand of me, I know I will have to work hard all the time. To hit this level I must be focused completely on my football. I could have stayed where I was comfortable, but what attracted me to Liverpool is it's a working team. The gaffer has put a mentality into the team that means everyone must work hard for success. This is known to be a key characteristic of Benitez's side and I like this.'

Fernando also revealed that another aspect of Liverpool that appealed to him was the city's working-class roots, believing as he did that clubs in areas like that shared a special affinity with the fans. It was a relationship he had clearly enjoyed with Atletico Madrid's supporters and he was obviously hoping to foster a similar one on Merseyside. 'I like that Liverpool is a working-class area with supporters who I believe are similar to those of Atletico, who appreciate and respect hard work,' he continued. 'At this kind of club, there is usually a special bond between the players and the supporters. It means there is a different spirit about the city and the club compared to some others. Although the players have told me about the mentality of the Liverpool people, and how the fans are, I don't think this is something which can be explained in words. It is only something I can understand when I play my first game at Anfield against Chelsea. Then I will fully know about the relationship between the Liverpool supporters and the players.'

His signing was seen as a massive coup for Liverpool and another step in the right direction as Benitez tried to build a title-winning squad and solve the puzzle of why his side seemed to excel in Europe but fall short in their own domestic competition. And Torres' arrival was welcomed with great enthusiasm by his new team-mates. Captain Steven Gerrard, who, as a born and bred Liverpudlian, fully understood the fans' frustration at the team's inability to challenge Manchester United and Chelsea for the Premier League crown, was absolutely ecstatic at the capture of the Spaniard. He said, 'Torres has all the attributes to become firmly established as world class. Some of the other players we're being linked with excite me, too. It's great to see us looking at young, hungry players with their best years ahead of them. Since I've been in the first team I can't remember us making such a major statement of intent in the transfer market as this. In recent years, it's only really been Manchester United and Chelsea buying players around the £20m mark, so it's great to see us able to compete for players of that kind of value.

'The Liverpool board has always backed the manager and we've invested heavily over the years. Roy Evans and Gerard Houllier spent a lot of money, but we've all been looking for that extra step to close the gap and attract the kind of players United and Chelsea are able to afford. This is the first summer in a long time we've been able to do that. I'll bet players and fans from other clubs have been looking at us and thinking, "Aye, aye, Liverpool are making a move for some of the big boys now." That's what's so exciting. When the American owners took over they talked about three stages. The first was proceeding with the new stadium, which they're doing; then they wanted to secure the key players on long-term contracts, which they've done. Stage three is all about spending money on the players to make us compete for the Premier League, which has now started. We're looking in great shape, not only going into this season, but for the next few years.'

And Gerrard was in no doubt that the club's record signing possessed all the attributes necessary to set English football alight. 'I've never played against him, but I've watched him a lot,' he added while talking to the club's website. 'I really like him and I'm sure he will prove a great signing for us. Not only is he a great player now, but potentially he has all the attributes to become firmly established as world class. He's at the right club and will be working with the right people to make that happen. He's a fast, strong centre-forward who likes the ball being played into his feet. They are the kind of strikers I love playing with. I've no doubt we're going to get our money's worth out of him, with him being such a young player.'

His Spanish team-mates at his new club, who, of course, knew more about him than most, were also convinced Liverpool had signed a proven match-winner. In an interview with the club's media department, midfield star Xabi Alonso said, 'I've known Torres, of course, since he first started playing in Spain. I think he can handle the pressure because he's experienced similar while at Atletico Madrid. Mentally, he is strong enough to deal with this. He knows there will be a lot of focus on him, particularly in the early days, but once he's scored his first goal that immediate pressure comes off.

'Fernando is someone who likes to work for his team. He always looks for the spaces and he's also someone who likes it [the ball] played into his feet, which is good for the midfielders because we can use different options when looking to pass to him. He is so quick he will cause a lot of problems for defenders. In the Premier League, the defenders are really strong, but I hope he will be able to get the better of them.

'We know Liverpool is different to other clubs, but that can be to his advantage. There are a lot of players here who've already achieved good things in the last few years, and it is our job to help him settle into the club as soon as possible. If we do that, it will allow him to show everyone what he's capable of.'

And goalkeeper Pepe Reina was backing his countryman to score the goals to fire Liverpool to glory. He insisted, 'We need a player that scores 20 or 25 goals a season and Fernando Torres can be that man. He has many virtues. I am confident that he will do very important things for the team. It's true that the style of football is different in England but we want him to be ready from the first minute and show the player he has been in recent years.

'Fernando will cause lots of problems for my fellow goalkeepers.

He's a great player and I'm sure the Liverpool fans are going to love him. The first year in a foreign country is always difficult but myself and all the other lads will be there for him every inch of the way to help him settle. Scoring goals will also help him settle and I can foresee no problems with him. He's a great lad. He's learning English early and has got the right mentality to succeed. I've spoken to him about a lot of things since he signed and I know he's ready for the challenge.'

Certainly, if Torres' performances on the pitch were as impressive as those off it, he would have no problems adapting to his new life in England. At his press conference to unveil him as a Liverpool player, he had worn a big smile throughout and won over the reporters with his easy-going manner. 'I don't care about the weather,' he insisted when asked about swapping the climate of Madrid for that of Merseyside, before adding, 'My girlfriend, who I will live with, is from Galicia, where it rains constantly!'

He also impressed Anfield fans by declining the opportunity to wear the new Atletico Madrid shirt on a trip back to his home city, believing that it would not be right to do so having just signed for another club. And, when the Atletico president moved to hug him, Fernando offered instead his hand as a gesture of farewell. All of this suggested a quiet dignity which augured well for his future prospects in England.

One difference he had noticed already during his short time in England was the intensity of the practice sessions compared to what he had been used to in Madrid. 'They do train here, don't they?' he said to Guillem Balague in an interview for *The Times* newspaper. But he understood the need for the high levels of fitness he would require to compete in what is widely regarded as being the fastest and most competitive league in the world. He added, 'I am going to play 20 more matches than at Atletico. But I am sure the adaptation is going to be easier partly because I know some of the guys here, but partly because I can already see in training that the team moves like a unit. It is a team that is already solid. I was running around trying to follow their moves but I'm still miles away from accomplishing that efficiently.

'But I can see I could be useful when we use the counter-attack, with the long balls of Gerrard or the passes from Xabi [Alonso]. It is up to me to give even more to the team. I have scored more goals when I have been playing as a target man, but I can play off another striker, do his dirty work if you like.

'I will have to get used to the different intensity of the Premier League. I also need to get rid of some of the habits one learns when younger. There will be a price to pay while I learn, a yellow card or two. At least I know from having watched the Premier League that referees allow more to the forward. In Spain, if I made a fault [a foul] it was a yellow card straight away, but here I can be physical.'

Torres began life as a Liverpool player on pre-season tours to Switzerland and Hong Kong as he got to know his new team-mates and a new way of playing. An ankle injury caused him some concerns and restricted his participation but, by the first game of the Rotterdam Tournament in early August, he was ready for his first start, with Shanghai Shenhua providing the perhaps unlikely opposition.

Throughout the build-up to the season, Torres had appeared relaxed, confident and comfortable in his new surroundings. 'I am very happy to be here working with the team. I respect and admire a lot of my Liverpool team-mates and can learn from them. They are well known all around the world. I was famous in Spain but I'd like to be famous throughout the world, just like they are,' he told a press gathering during the tour of Hong Kong. And he also demonstrated his art at avoiding the pitfalls the media can sometimes place in front of players when answering 'the more the better' when quizzed about his goalscoring targets for the season, before adding, 'Scoring goals is not just about me. All the team have to work together.'

Within 12 minutes of his full debut, he proved that the burden of carrying the club's goalscoring hopes was one he could cope with. After taking a pass from Yossi Benayoun in his stride, he finished in style by clipping the ball over the Shanghai goalkeeper to give Liverpool the lead. Liverpool went on to win the game 2–0, with substitute Steven Gerrard grabbing the second goal, but it was the performance of Torres that most excited Liverpool's management and supporters. Boss Benitez said, 'Getting off the mark will give Torres a lot of confidence heading into the new season. I was very pleased with Fernando, it was very important for him to score his first goal for Liverpool. He has had chances in every game he has played in pre-season, and for him to get this first goal is great for his confidence. I remember when Peter Crouch first joined us and everyone was asking when he was going to score. Torres has now got that and that takes the pressure off.'

And the player himself was equally happy to have opened his

scoring account for his new club. He told liverpoolfc.tv, 'I'm very pleased to have scored my first goal. I'm happy with that and with the victory for the team. I hope that it will be the first of many. Right now, I'm going to enjoy this moment. I intend to score lots of goals and, when the league starts, that's where they will be the most important.'

It was clear that Torres was already slotting neatly into Liverpool's intended pattern of play for the new season, and he was quick to pay tribute to his team-mates for aiding his transition into the team. 'It's good with my team-mates', he continued. 'I'm enjoying everything about this great club and with the great players it has I can learn a lot and have been since my very first day. It's all new for me but I'm learning more and adapting to playing in the team. Some things are made easier in one way because everyone is doing everything they can and everything possible in order for me to adapt and settle in quickly. It's the same both on and off the pitch... they are all supporting me and giving me a hand and I'm so lucky because with people like that it's much easier.'

Liverpool ended the Rotterdam Tournament in second place after drawing 1–1 with hosts Feyenoord in their second match, meaning Porto took the trophy on goal difference after beating Shanghai Shenhua 3–0, but the pre-season preparations were certainly continuing along the right lines. And, with the new season just a week away, Torres was in confident mood as he contemplated his first match in the Premier League. 'I know that in this competition the four top teams are all capable of taking the Premier League so every point is important and we must have that attitude from the start,' he said. 'The truth is I'm so happy that I came here. Every day that goes by I'm learning more and more about the special story and history of this great club and how much it means to the fans. They are so passionate and have high expectations, so obviously I want to give everything I can to live up to those expectations.

'I can promise to give everything. This is one of the greatest clubs in the world and I want to learn and I want to win. It will without doubt take a lot of work but I will do everything that I can.'

4

RED HOT

Fernando Torres, it was hoped on Merseyside, would be the missing piece in Rafael Benitez's jigsaw, the one that would make whole the sum of the parts and finally deliver the Premier League trophy to Anfield. If that should be the case, that record price tag would have been a small one to pay.

The young Spaniard's debut for his new club was to be away at Aston Villa and there was naturally much expectation surrounding his first game in the Premier League. Would he live up to the hype? Could he deliver under pressure? Would he really be able to cope with the physical demands of the most demanding league in the world?

They were all valid questions but, just as he had done when he made the step up from the junior ranks into the senior ranks with Atletico Madrid, Torres was to prove that he was more than capable of thriving on any stage.

And certainly, as he approached his introduction to English football at Villa Park, his manager was in no doubt that he would be anything other than an unmitigated success. And he stressed that, if opposing defenders wanted to concentrate primarily on putting the new recruit off his game, then so much the better for his team-mates. Benitez told a news conference on the eve of the Villa game, 'If people want to talk only about Fernando, he can handle this and it may work to our advantage because they may forget how good our other players are. It will be good for the other players if all the attention is on Fernando. Maybe Voronin, Babel or Benayoun will feel there is less pressure on them. Or maybe Crouch, Kuyt and Voronin will take advantage if defenders are thinking they must stop Torres. If the attention is always on Fernando, it's good for the rest of our team.'

Benitez also revealed that the Spanish international was bursting to get into the action and see for himself what English football was all about. He added, 'I know he's a little nervous because he's excited about playing his first real game for Liverpool. He's particularly looking forward to playing at Anfield for the first time next week because he's heard so much about the fans and the atmosphere. Our supporters will be patient with Fernando. Maybe those outside our club won't be because they will want to keep more pressure on him for as long as possible, but the important thing is we know he has the determination to be successful over a long period.

'There is always pressure in football, but he knows this because he was an icon at Atletico Madrid, so it won't be too different for him and there will be a lot of people here and good players to help him. He will need time, but every new player in England needs time.

'He's also used to being targeted by defenders, but he can handle this, too. He's a strong boy. He's been talking a lot about this first game and we know he's ready.'

Liverpool made the perfect start to the new campaign, beating Villa 2–1 thanks to Gerrard's late winner and, although Torres did not get off the mark with a goal, he showed enough class to leave his manager more than satisfied. Benitez paired his new signing with Dirk Kuyt in attack and was full of praise for their performances. He said, 'I was happy with what Fernando did. He worked very hard. He and Kuyt were a problem for their defenders. That was the idea.

'The movement and understanding was good and he [Torres] showed the touches and class that I would expect from him. Normally, players when they arrive need a little time to settle in but the understanding with Kuyt was good from the start. I took him [Torres] off with 20 minutes to go and it was difficult for me to decide which player to change. I just felt it was going to give us some fresh legs at the end of the game.'

Strike partner Kuyt was also quick to salute his new team-mate, saying, 'I don't think Fernando needs too many games [before he finds his best form]. He is top quality and with a bit more luck at Villa he would have scored his first goal. I think myself and Fernando had a few chances and I thought we looked good together. The teamwork for that first goal was really good and we just tried to keep going.'

It was a hugely encouraging start for Torres and one former Liverpool striker had already seen enough to be convinced that the club had struck gold in the transfer market by signing the Spaniard.

On the eve of the new boy's Anfield debut against Chelsea, John Aldridge told the club's website, 'As a former striker I was watching Fernando Torres' performance very closely at Aston Villa and I liked what I saw. His all-round attributes were excellent. In fact, I saw similarities in his performance to that of one of his opponents tomorrow, Didier Drogba.

'A key part of Chelsea's success has been their ability to play balls to the front men and see them make something out of nothing. Torres did this on several occasions last weekend. He could have taken a few chances but he had no right to have them in the first place because he made most of those opportunities for himself.

'I liked the way he held the ball up, put himself about, chased down defenders and wanted to get on the end of everything. The link-up play with Dirk Kuyt was also excellent. There are already signs of a flourishing partnership which is something Liverpool have lacked for years.

'I see Peter Crouch and Torres working just as well together. While Kuyt can play as a foil for Torres, the Spaniard would play a different role alongside Crouch and probably help Peter play further up the park. It's still early days but there are so many options available for Rafa now, it bodes well for the rest of the season.'

Liverpool approached the visit of Chelsea, a huge early test of their title credentials, on the back of two successive wins and full of confidence, having followed up their opening-day victory at Aston Villa with a 1–0 success over Toulouse in the qualifying rounds of the Champions League. So it was a buoyant and excited Torres who faced the media ahead of the clash with the Blues. He had sat out the midweek game against the French, but there was no way Benitez was going to deny him the home debut he so craved.

Torres said, 'Last Saturday was my Premier League debut and we came away with the win; on Wednesday it was the Champions League and we also won; and on Sunday I will walk out at Anfield for the first time to play a match.

'Everybody tells me that until I listen to "You'll Never Walk Alone" inside our stadium it's as if I've never really heard it properly, and I can't wait to hear it.'

And the striker also confessed that in the short time he had been on Merseyside his priorities for the season had already started to shift. He admitted, 'The Champions League is the lucky competition for Liverpool and it's a tradition. But it's curious that I came here thinking about the Champions League because it's a special competition for me, but in the team everybody is thinking about the Premier League.

'It must be because many of them won in Istanbul [against AC Milan in the 2005 Champions League final] but they've never won the league. By the way, neither have I. The club hasn't done it for 17 years and here everyone believes this could be the year.'

If the players and fans felt that way before the game against Chelsea, those beliefs were fully reinforced against the Blues. Liverpool were desperately unlucky not to win the game and could feel harshly done by that Chelsea escaped with a point after Frank Lampard converted from the penalty spot following the award of a spot-kick by referee Rob Styles for an innocuous clash between Steve Finnan and Florent Malouda. But once the anger and bitterness at that decision subsided, it was the impact of Torres that was the subject of much excited chatter around the pubs and clubs of Liverpool.

The Spaniard had opened the scoring after 16 minutes of the match, squaring up to Chelsea defender Tal Ben Haim and then gliding past him as if he were not there, before finishing with aplomb with a neat side-footed finish across goalkeeper Petr Cech and into the far corner. It was a moment to savour for the new recruit and one he would never forget.

Benitez insisted after the match that the striker's unerring finish proved that the Reds were right to fork out a record transfer fee to sign him during the close season. 'The players know now that Torres has pace and he can score the goals that we need,' said the Liverpool manager. 'Fernando showed pace and quality, he scored a great goal for us and the supporters. He learned a lot from the game but it is still too early to judge him. He will need a little more time. He was playing against the best defenders in England and he had no problems. I am very pleased and for the future it was positive. He showed the quality he has and we will see more goals from him.'

Meanwhile, Torres himself, while clearly delighted with a goal on his home debut, was quick to warn his adoring new fans not to expect too much too soon and to reiterate that he still had a lot to learn about the game in England. 'Everything is different in England and I have to get used to that,' said the Spaniard. 'The way the fans live the game and sing throughout to create an atmosphere is different. Before the game, everyone sings as well. It is not the same as it is in Spain.

'The English game is more physical, too, but it's nice. It's end to end, it flows more and it doesn't stop so often. For the fans and for the players, that's great.

'Manchester United and Chelsea are the strongest teams, but every game is intense. You have to adapt your game according to your opponents. There is a lot of expectation among the fans because of the fee, but all I can do is work hard and score goals like I did against Chelsea. Scoring helps with your adaptation, but I don't feel any pressure, so the goal did not come as a relief.'

His immediate impact in English football was a huge bonus for the Reds and it had former players queuing up to eulogise the man who already looked destined to carve his name into Liverpool folklore. Just as Aldridge had been effusive in his praise the week before, now two more former Anfield heroes, who had been instrumental in the club's extraordinary success in the 1980s, were bursting with admiration for the new signing. Legendary goalscorer Ian Rush said, 'Torres couldn't have done any more to win over the Liverpool supporters against Chelsea. His goal reminded me of a young Michael Owen, with lightning pace and a perfect finish. When you have a striker with that kind of speed, it's a major asset for any team. But just being fast isn't enough. You need to be quick off the mark to make the most of your qualities, and, if you add the kind of awareness and finishing ability we saw on Sunday into the mix, it's some combination.

'The manner in which he side-footed the ball into the one corner of the net where Petr Cech had no chance of saving it proved Liverpool have signed a class act. I also like the way Torres works so hard for the team. The Kop have found an instant hero. After scoring against Chelsea, Torres should have the confidence to take on everyone.'

Those were sentiments shared by Rush's former partner in goals, Kenny Dalglish. The ex-Scotland international great had watched Torres' Anfield debut on TV in Spain and he certainly liked what he saw, particularly the newcomer's controlled aggression. 'I was off my seat in Spain when he stood up to John Terry in the first half when Terry was screaming in his face,' Dalglish told *LFC* magazine. 'That's what you want to see from your players – he wasn't aggressive or annoyed, he just showed Terry he wasn't bothered by what he did. He got up and stood his ground. He refused to be intimidated but made sure he kept his hands by his sides. There's not many people disturb John Terry's calm but Torres did it inside the first ten minutes.

'I was delighted for him when he scored. The way the boy anticipated what Stevie [Gerrard] was going to do with the ball, and then the clever way he stopped and then started his marker tells you he's going to be a star. You'd better believe that just about every central defender in the country will have been tuned into that game, and they'll all be nervous about facing him, maybe even frightened.'

And, on the evidence of just the first couple of Premier League games of the season, Rush was backing the Reds to be a major force in the title race and finally sustain a challenge to Manchester United and Chelsea. 'If Chelsea and Manchester United didn't already consider Liverpool serious title contenders, they do now,' stressed the Welshman on the Liverpool website. 'Sunday's performance [against Chelsea] underlined why Liverpool can go closer this season than at any time in the last 17 years.'

'There's very little to choose between Rafa's team and José

Mourinho's side now. The gap that's been there has shrunk, although the genuine test may come at venues such as the Stadium of Light next weekend as much as at Stamford Bridge or Old Trafford later in the season.'

The argument Rush was making was that the next task facing Liverpool was to find the consistency that has been the hallmark of sides like Manchester United and Chelsea in recent seasons. The Reds needed to find the right ingredients to deliver the goods against all opposition, not just step up to the mark in the so-called big games. By performing so well against Chelsea they had proved they had the mettle to deliver on the big stage, now they needed to develop the habit of overwhelming lesser opponents. Only by marrying the two attributes could they hope to succeed over the course of a long, hard Premier League season.

For now, though, Rush and all Liverpool fans were encouraged by what they had seen so far and, with a relatively inviting fixture list in the early weeks of the season, there was genuine optimism around Anfield that the team could lay down a marker for the coming months.

'There's no reason why Liverpool can't begin the season with an impressive, unbeaten run,' continued Rush. 'They now look as if they have what it takes.'

It was a terrific start for Torres and the team as a whole but, while the plaudits continued to rain down on the head of the man who would be king, Benitez was quick to sound a note of caution to those who were already comparing the young Spaniard to greats such as Dalglish. He said, 'If Fernando can play at the same level as Kenny Dalglish it would be amazing. Dalglish was a fantastic player, but

Fernando will need time. It was important for him to score his first goal and to score such a great goal in front of your own supporters in a big game was even more important.

'He has shown he is good enough, but don't expect him to score a goal every week. Yes, he's capable of doing good things and he's a good prospect, but he needs to keep working and improving. He needs time and our support to do these things.'

But, while refusing to go overboard about the then 23-year-old, Benitez was prepared to admit that it appeared as though he had brought a missing ingredient to the Liverpool side. 'It's a big difference for us to have a player like Fernando, a player who can score big goals in big games,' added the Anfield boss. 'He has experience at international level, too, and for the team it's important to have a player who can score and change the game, even when you're not playing well.

'When we decided to bring him here we analysed a lot of things and one of those was his mentality. We found that he has a very good mentality and can cope with pressure. He can play with big names and not be afraid.'

Liverpool's excellent start to the season continued as they made it four wins out of five by beating Sunderland 2–0 at the Stadium of Light – a perfect response to Rush's assertion that the Reds should be winning these 'lesser' games – and finishing the qualification job against Toulouse with a convincing 4–0 win at Anfield to confirm their place in the Champions League group stages. That was followed by a crushing 6–0 Anfield win against Premier League newcomers Derby, a game in which Torres once again proved his predatory instincts, netting two more goals to leave his manager, team-mates and the media all purring about his latest starring performance.

The Liverpool *Daily Post* described his display by saying, 'Torres in particular caught the eye, the Spain striker continuing his seamless introduction into English football with a powerful display which brought him a second-half double. More than any of the summer captures, the 23-year-old has transformed Benitez's men as an attacking force, adding pace, strength and guile to the Spaniard's forward line. Torres' appetite for graft has also helped the marksman to settle quickly into life in the Premier League.'

Midfielder Alonso, who also helped himself to two goals in the rout, was similarly hugely impressed with his team-mate's sparkling show against the Rams. He said, 'I think Fernando is doing really well. He has settled into the Premier League very quickly and that is encouraging because it can be difficult coming into a new league. He has great pace, physical strength and hopefully he will score more goals now.

'He has shown he is not afraid of the physical contact here, with defenders trying to put him off, and that is really important. You can see he is not afraid. Defenders will realise that he is not scared and it is like a motivation for him. He seems to like the challenge of trying to come out on top and he is doing really well for us.'

Benitez, too, was equally pleased with his new star signing but, while some people may have been shocked by Torres' early impact, he insisted that he was not at all surprised by how well he was playing or how quickly he had settled into life in England. The Anfield boss told reporters, 'We knew he had power and movement which would suit the Premier League. He's scoring goals, playing well and his understanding with the others is really good. We already knew he was really strong and he will be even stronger in a few months as well. He's working really hard.'

It was not only in England that his impact was being noticed though. Back in Spain they were also intrigued to see how Torres was faring in a new environment. And one former rival reckoned the move had done the Spaniard the world of good. Real Madrid legend Raul said of Fernando, 'He was an icon at Atletico Madrid and had to make a personal decision [to leave], one that I respect. There is a different air about him now, and it looks like he is enjoying the experience.

'I watched his debut against Aston Villa on television, and I also saw his great goal against Chelsea. There can be no doubt that he has taken an important step in the right direction. He gave a lot to Atletico Madrid, and this is a new challenge, though I am sure that he will triumph. With a good coach like Rafa Benitez, and with the help of his Spanish team-mates [at Anfield], the process of adaptation will be easier. There is no doubt that he will do well.'

There was certainly no doubt he was doing well so far and the player himself could not have been happier with the early days of his new career in England. And already it appeared his mind was made up that he would remain at Anfield for the foreseeable future. 'I am learning quickly and my team-mates have played an important role, along with everyone at the club who have all gone out of their way to help me,' he said. 'I feel as if I have been at Liverpool for a long time. I intend to stay here for many years to come and I am really pleased with everything – my new team-mates, the fans, the city, the stadium.

'After I left Atletico Madrid, I dreamed of days like I had against Derby. It was a magic Saturday and I know it is early but I have confidence we can carry on playing like this. Scoring two goals at Anfield in the Premier League shows that I am ready for this big challenge.

'Everything this summer, all the hard work in making the move happen, has been proved worthwhile by games like this. My objective now is to be an idol at Liverpool and if I keep scoring goals like this then hopefully it will help me become a favourite for the fans.

'I know that many people have doubted me because of the size of the transfer fee but my answer will always be with the goals I score. That is the most important thing in the world, especially for me as a striker who feeds on goals.'

And, while he was not quite prepared to set himself a definitive target in terms of a goals return, he was certainly aiming reasonably high. He added, 'I don't want to set a target but if I avoid injuries and stay in good form then I want a minimum of 15 goals. That will be a good number for me in what will be a very hard first season in the Premier League.' Little did he suspect then that he would dwarf that target as he took the English game by storm in the months to come.

It had been a dream first month for him in English football, scoring three goals in his first four Premier League games, and it can have come as no surprise when Liverpool fans voted him as the club's star performer for August. A poll on the club's official website saw Torres glean 42 per cent of the overall vote, three times as many as

Jermaine Pennant, who came in second with 14 per cent. It was yet another ringing endorsement of the player's talents and further proof that the Reds' fans had taken him immediately to their hearts.

It had been a fantastic start to his career in domestic English football, but next on the horizon for Liverpool was the start of the Champions League group stages and, for Torres, finally the chance to play on European club football's greatest stage.

He had openly admitted that the lure of Champions League football was one of the reasons he finally made the decision to quit Atletico Madrid and now here he was, about to make his first appearance in the competition. As he prepared for the first match of the tournament proper, away to Porto, he admitted to reporters, 'Everyone wants to play in Europe, to be among the greats. I did not come here because of money, I came for the challenge and the chance to win things and I believe I can do that with Liverpool. The chance to play in the Champions League and with great players is what matters. I want to contribute with my goals.'

It was a clear statement of intent from the striker and one that was endorsed by manager Benitez, who fully expected his record signing to make a similar impact on the European stage to the one he had made at domestic level. Benitez said, 'The chance to show his talents in the Champions League was one of the reasons he decided to come to a top side. He wanted to play in Europe at the highest level. Mentally he is ready for this challenge. When you can play as well as he has done in the Premier League then you can play in Europe, no problems.

'He is only young, 23, but the problem was he had been in the

Atletico Madrid team since he was 17 and was waiting, waiting for them to get into the Champions League. Now he has the opportunity to show what he can do at this level.'

In the end, it was not a great night for Liverpool in Portugal as they were forced to defend for long periods of the second half following Jermaine Pennant's red card 12 minutes after the break. But they held on for a point in a 1–1 draw, never the worst start to a European campaign when your first game is away from home.

Unfortunately for Torres, his first game in the Champions League had not gone entirely to plan. When he next made his debut in a cup competition, however, he could not have wished for a better outcome as he fired home a hat-trick, his first for Liverpool, in a 4–2 Carling Cup win over Reading at the Madejski Stadium.

It was another virtuoso performance by the striker, perhaps justifying Benitez's decision to start with him on the bench in the previous two Premier League games as his much-talked-about rotation policy came under scrutiny again.

Certainly, that was a point not lost on radio commentator Steve Hothersall, who told listeners to Radio City, 'Fernando Torres was absolutely special, especially with the way he responded to the two Reading defenders who were trying to bully him off the ball at every opportunity. He showed pure class with the way he just picked himself up from their brutality and punished them with a hat-trick of the highest quality.

'Maybe Rafa was right to rest him for the last two Premier League games because he produced a special performance, and he might just now go on and score a lot more goals in the Premier League. One thing is clear and that is Liverpool have a truly special talent in Fernando Torres.'

That was a sentiment clearly shared by the Anfield faithful. One entry on the club website's message board, posted by Blue-eyedKopGirl, summed up the feelings of many supporters: 'Finally, a player to justify the number 9 shirt.'

And it was not just outsiders looking in who were effusive in their praise of the Spaniard. Peter Crouch, who played up front alongside Torres at the Madejski Stadium, insisted, 'He was magnificent at Reading. The thing about Fernando is that he's a top-class player but he works so hard for the team. You can see that. The manager obviously likes all the players to work hard and the strikers to track back – he does that extremely well, as well as his more obvious qualities.

'His goals were fantastically taken and it was a superb all-round performance. He's a strong lad and he proved that he can certainly cope with the physical side. He comes from a different way of playing – Spanish football is different to English football – but he's an extremely strong physical player. He has pace and attributes to help him cope with that. I'm sure he's going to be a force this year.'

And defender Jamie Carragher was also able to appreciate the efforts of his new team-mate, adding, 'It was his first hat-trick and hopefully there'll be a few more. He won us a tight game. The difference was his pace, especially in the second half. There were some great finishes, but it's not just his goals, it's his all-round work-rate. He's a real team player. If he doesn't score he's still there closing people down, putting the graft in and making it difficult for people. He's made a great start to his Liverpool career and long may it continue.'

It had been a better start to his Anfield career than surely even Fernando could have hoped for. Goals under his belt, the fans on his side and the media singing his praises, all of a sudden that near-£27m record fee was beginning to look like a bargain. But Fernando, while obviously confident of his own natural talents and abilities, was quick to point out that his transition into English football had been aided by a personalised training plan that had been drawn up by Benitez and his staff to help to try to ensure a smooth transition from La Liga to the Premier League.

Such is the meticulous attention to detail at Anfield that the staff had left no stone unturned in their efforts to help Torres adapt to English football. But it was not only the Spaniard who was expected to follow a strict practice regime, it applied to the whole squad. Training varies from week to week and is geared towards the strength and weaknesses of the team's next opponents and specific moves are repeated and practised over and over again to try to ensure perfection on the day.

As well as the extra vigilance on the training ground paying off, it was also clear that Torres was relishing Liverpool's style of play. At Atletico, he had often found himself having to drop deep into the midfield to look for the ball himself, and that extra work load naturally blunted his effectiveness in the final third. At Liverpool, though, he was surrounded by players whose task it was to do that unglamorous work in the middle of the park, freeing him to do the job for which the club had bought him, attacking the opposition at pace on the counter-attack. Already it was evident that the direct nature of English football would suit his style and the runs he loves to make in behind defences.

The next task for Liverpool was to use that result against Reading as a springboard to reignite their Premier League campaign, having stuttered to 0–0 draws in their previous two matches against Portsmouth and Birmingham. Fernando admitted, 'We all realise that we have let slip some points in our last two games and that we cannot continue to do this if we want to be in the fight for the title.'

For long-suffering Liverpool fans, that was becoming a familiar tale. But it was a story they hoped their team would be able to rewrite this season, particularly with Torres now installed as the focal point of their attack.

The Reds went some way to redressing the balance in the next game, claiming a 1–0 win at Wigan, but the free-flowing convincing football they had played at the start of the season, form that had convinced so many pundits and critics alike that Benitez had finally hit upon a winning formula, had mysteriously deserted them. That was a situation that was clearly troubling Benitez, but the Anfield chief was equally perplexed at some of the treatment being meted out by Premier League defenders to Torres. And he called for referees to stamp down on the offenders and protect his player. He said, 'What puzzles me is why people are talking all the time about Torres [being brave] when he plays, when they should surely be talking about how we can protect him when he plays.

'There was lots of talk about how Torres coped so well [against Reading] ... I'm surprised people aren't talking about the need to

Torres in action for Spain's winning team at the 2001 UEFA Under-16 Championship.

© PA Photos

Torres was still in his teens when he began to make a name for himself in the first team of his beloved Atletico Madrid.

© PA Photo

Above: Torres helped Spain to qualify for Euro 2004, his first major international tournament.

Below: Showing a clean pair of heels to Ukraine's Sergei Federov during that qualification campaign.

© *PA Photos*

Above: Torres in pensive mood during a training session at Euro 2004 in Portugal.

Below: A good start at Euro 2004 as Spain beat Russia in their opening match, with Torres appearing as a late substitute for Raul.

© *PA Photo*

Leading the line for his country against Greece at Euro 2004.

© *PA Photos*

Hair today, gone tomorrow! Despite Torres' best efforts, Spain lost to Portugal in their third group game at Euro 2004 and left the tournament before the knockout stages. © PA Photos

Above: Torres scores against Belgium in a World Cup qualifier in October 2005.

Below: A thoughtful Torres faces the media before Spain's play-off match against Slovakia in November 2005, with a place at the World Cup in Germany at stake.   © *PA Photos*

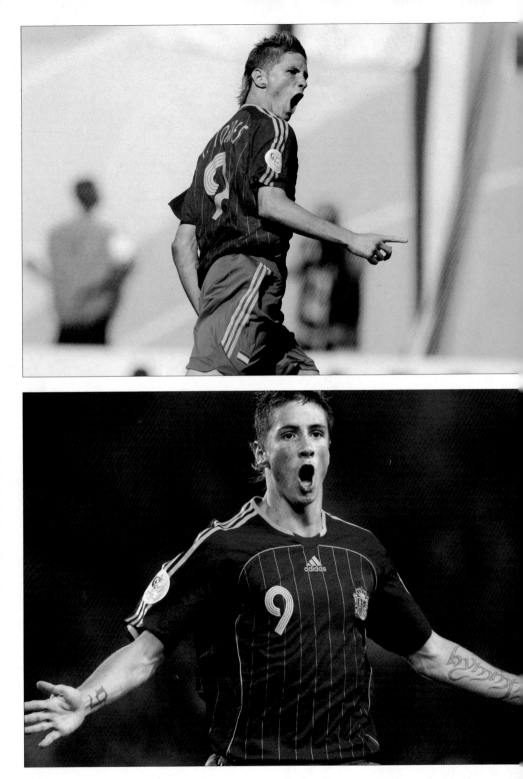

Above: Torres and Spain make the perfect start at the 2006 World Cup, beating Ukraine 4–0 in their opening group game.

Below: Torres celebrates a goal against Tunisia in a comfortable 3–1 win for Spain to book their place in the second phase in Germany.

© *Rex Feature*

protect players of quality, because, if we want to see exciting matches with real quality for the fans, then we must ensure the quality players are allowed to play ...'

If the manager's mood had been soured by some rough-house treatment dished out to Torres and a less than convincing run of league results, then it was to be darkened still further when Liverpool made an uncharacteristic slip-up in the Champions League in their next outing, at home to Marseille. Benitez had prided himself on his success in Europe during his Anfield reign and, in many ways, those glory nights had rather disguised the fact that, if truth be told, the team appeared no nearer bridging the gap between themselves and the likes of Manchester United and Chelsea at the top of the Premier League than they had on the day he took charge. But, by winning the Champions League in 2005 and reaching the final again in 2007, Benitez had proved that he was a master tactician when it came to pitting his wits against the best that Europe had to offer.

So it was a major surprise when Liverpool slumped to a home defeat to the Frenchmen and left their campaign on the brink of disaster, with just one point gained from their first two matches. Clearly, it was not the start they had been looking for.

For Torres, however, there was a personal accolade to enjoy amid the mild outbreak of doom and gloom at Anfield as he was nominated in a 30-strong list for FIFA's World Player of the Year award. It was a fitting reward for his efforts in his final months in Madrid and his first couple of months on Merseyside, as well as for the impact he was having for Spain in their Euro 2008 qualifying campaign.

He wrote warmly of his nomination for this prestigious award in an entry on his official website: 'I feel flattered at being nominated for the FIFA World Player. It is a proud moment for me, and an incentive to keep on working hard.'

The first thing at which he had to work hard was proving his fitness. Having signed off for Liverpool before linking up with the Spanish squad with a last-minute equaliser at home to Spurs to salvage a point in a 2–2 draw, he had returned to the club with a muscle tear sustained on international duty. And it could scarcely have come at a worse time as it put in jeopardy his chances of playing in his first Merseyside derby against Everton, Liverpool's first game following the two-week international break.

It was a game Fernando was determined to be ready for, as he told Spanish radio station EFE: 'I intend to be fit,' he insisted. 'I don't want to miss out on the derby against Everton. I've been told how special the game is and I need to be ready in time. I am very happy at Liverpool and I've learned a lot – I love being at a big club like this. I have played in big derby matches before. I played for Atletico against Real Madrid and I'm looking forward to enjoying something similar in the Premier League.'

Try as he might, however, the injury proved to be too serious. It was his first setback during his time in England and came at a particularly bad time for Liverpool as they continued to struggle to find their best form. Although they won the Merseyside derby 2–1 at Everton, thanks to two penalties from Dirk Kuyt, the second of which came in the very last minute, they were still lacking their early season cohesion.

And their season was about to take a potentially catastrophic turn for the worse as they travelled to Turkey to face Besiktas in their third Champions League qualifying match. The Turks were widely regarded as the group's whipping boys and Liverpool were expected to claim a comfortable victory in the city where they so famously won the tournament on that unforgettable night in Istanbul two-and-a-half years earlier.

But there was to be no fairytale ending this time as the Reds slumped to a 2–1 defeat. They had 28 attempts on goal during the course of the 90 minutes and enjoyed almost 60 per cent of the possession, but they had only Steven Gerrard's late goal to show for their dominance, not enough to cancel out Sami Hyypia's first-half own-goal and a strike from Bobo.

That result left Liverpool clinging to their European hopes by their fingernails, knowing that they would need to win all three of their remaining group games to stand any chance of qualification. And even then they might be relying on other results to go their way. For Liverpool, the Champions League knockout matches would begin well before Christmas.

On a brighter note, Torres was passed fit to return to first-team action for the next Premier League match at home to Arsenal. The bad news, though, was that he lasted just 45 minutes of the 1–1 draw before having to withdraw injured with a recurrence of his muscle strain.

And this time the injury was more serious. A scan revealed a tear to a different abductor muscle from the original injury and it was expected he would be out of action for three weeks.

It was an unhappy Fernando Torres who told the club's website, 'It's terrible. I'm the sort of player who misses two games a season at most through injury, so it's a very strange situation for me. I hate it when I'm not playing games. I'm certainly not used to it. Now I know how the fans feel when they're watching us play. You see so much from the stands that you can't appreciate when you're involved in the match. I suffered when we were going through difficult periods against Everton and Besiktas, so, yes, I'd much rather be out there than in the stands.'

While his injury may have left him depressed, however, he was far happier with the decision he had made in the summer to leave Madrid for Merseyside. Four months into his new life in England, he was already settled and contented and happily contemplating fulfilling his entire six-year contract and insisting he did not yearn for his home country. 'I am going to complete my contract with Liverpool at the very least,' he told Spanish radio station Radio Marca. 'I am comfortable at this great club. Here you are respected as a great player. You are going to grounds with the feeling that you are going to win. I am not planning to return to Spain, not now nor for many years.

'The support of the fans has been phenomenal. Here the people see you on the street and they greet you like a friend. In the stadia, when you are substituted at a rival ground, the public applauds you. It is certainly a different way of seeing football for me.'

All he wanted at that time, however, was to get back on to the pitch and into the thick of the action. And he was determined to do all he could to defy the doctors who had prescribed a three-week rest period, saying, 'People are talking about three or four weeks but

I've got to hope it will be sooner than that. Let's hope I'll be in perfect condition to play soon and that will be an end to the injuries this season. But I've got to make sure I'm absolutely right so it [the injury] doesn't return.'

In the end, he missed two weeks and three games – a Carling Cup fourth-round win over Cardiff, a 0–0 Premier League draw against Blackburn and a thumping 8–0 home win over Besiktas as Liverpool finally got their Champions League campaign back on track. And when he did return, for the home game against Fulham, he wasted no time in showing everyone what the side had been missing in his absence. With the game heading for a 0–0 draw and more frustration for Liverpool in their league title challenge, the Spaniard was introduced into the fray, as a substitute for Andriy Voronin, with 19 minutes remaining.

And he had been on the pitch for just ten of those minutes when he scored a stunning goal, controlling Pepe Reina's long goal-kick and cutting inside Aaron Hughes before firing home at the near post. It was a special goal and set the Reds on the way to a victory they secured with another late goal from Steven Gerrard from the penalty spot.

But it was Fernando who took all the post-match plaudits. Benitez told journalists, 'It was good to see Fernando come back and score a really good goal. The idea was to keep him on the bench and if we needed something we knew he was there and the supporters would always be behind him.

'Fernando's goal was very good, real quality. But when we signed him we knew he could do things like this. Goals like that are what you pay big money for. It was great quality and showed tremendous skill. It is what you expect from a player of his value.'

That was a view seconded in many quarters of the media, summed up neatly by Paul Joyce of the *Daily Express*, who wrote, 'Torres proved the old adage of you get what you pay for. He not only saps the confidence of the opposition but he lifts the Liverpool team with his presence. His goal was absolutely top drawer and his speed and power is fantastic. In my opinion, he can go on to be one of the great strikers for Liverpool over many years to come.'

Liverpool followed up their win against Fulham with a convincing 3–0 victory at Newcastle, cementing their place in the top five, six points behind the early-season leaders Arsenal. And it left Torres in a buoyant and bullish mood, convinced that the club were well placed to make a sustained championship challenge. Although everyone at the club accepted that the side had not yet hit peak performance, the fact that they were in the leading pack augured well for the months ahead. And it was a fact not lost on the Spaniard as he settled into English football.

'From what I have seen so far in England, we do not have anything to fear from any of our opponents for the title,' he told the Liverpool FC website. 'They are all great teams with a lot of experience and many very, very good players...but so are we. I am sure that as the season progresses it will come down to a fight between Manchester United, Arsenal and Chelsea – and we will be in there, too.'

Torres' belief in his new team-mates was unquestionable and it was a belief that stemmed from being around the players and the coaching staff day in, day out, observing their quality and recognising that there was a winning mentality at the club, something he was arguably not used to. While at Atletico he would look around the dressing room and see players hoping to win, at Liverpool he saw players expecting to win – a crucial difference at the very top level of professional sport where mental strength is such a vital component.

Their attitude, that failure was not an option, was rubbing off on Torres and he was also starting to approach games in far more confident fashion. And he was sure that, if Liverpool were able to keep their players fit, they could build a momentum that would make them very hard to stop, particularly given their impressive defensive record.

'Any team that concedes as few goals as we concede is going to be tough to play against,' he added. 'If we begin to take the chances that we are creating in our games then I am sure those teams above us will start to fear us.'

However, before Fernando and his team-mates could begin to apply yet more pressure to the teams above them in the Premier League table, they had to continue their challenge in Europe. The next visitors to Anfield were Porto for another game the Reds simply had to win. And win they did, in style.

Torres netted the first two goals, and Gerrard and Crouch scored one apiece to make the final scoreline a convincing 4–1. Having lost two of their first three games in the competition, they had recovered in fine style and now, with one match remaining in Marseille, they knew a win would secure a place in the last 16.

Torres' double strike took his tally to ten in his first 16 games for his new club and left his team-mates once more hailing him as the best in the business. Defender Jamie Carragher said, 'He is a world-class striker and he's probably up there with anyone now in striking terms. He's got raw pace and strength and that will cause defences problems. He looks like becoming the 20-goal-a-season striker we've been crying out for.' Thankfully, I only have to mark him in training!'

Another man who saw him every day up close and personal was goalkeeper Pepe Reina. Unlike Carragher, though, he knew what it was like to face Torres for real, having played against him during their days in Spain. And, while he agreed with the side's defensive linchpin that their team-mate was already among the world's best, he reckoned there was plenty more to come. 'Fernando has been in good form for the last two or three weeks and he is becoming an important player for us,' said Reina. 'He has got pace, he is finishing his chances well now, and he is still only 23. He has the qualities to play at a high level at the very top of English football because he is quick, he is strong, he is clever, has brilliant movement and is aggressive against big defenders. He is a target player who gives us a lot of things. Now let's see if he can get even better.

'Sometimes it can take time to adapt to playing in a different league, but Fernando has found it easier than some of the other players. It's important for him to keep on learning, and he's still only 23 so there is a long way to go for him. I played many times against him in Spain and I think I am one of his favourite goalkeepers because I have conceded many goals against him, but thankfully he is becoming my friend now!'

With the challenge from Porto successfully seen off, Liverpool's attention turned once again to the Premier League. With back-to-back wins against Fulham and Newcastle, the Reds had got themselves back on track following two successive draws. And they made it a comfortable three wins out of three in domestic competition as they hammered struggling Bolton 4–0 at Anfield. Torres claimed his side's second goal on the stroke of half-time to make the game safe, and further strikes from Steven Gerrard and Ryan Babel, to add to Sami Hyypia's early goal, gave the final scoreline a very convincing feel.

It was a terrific win against opponents Liverpool have often found tough to beat down the years and was a further indication that they appeared to be on the right lines to finally mount that sustained title challenge the fans had been craving for so long.

And that challenge looked like it was being built firmly on the foundations of what was becoming a magnificent partnership between Torres and Gerrard. Former Liverpool player Phil Neal, a man who won nine League Championship medals during his time at Anfield, said after the Bolton victory, 'Liverpool are great to watch at the moment and it's absolutely fantastic. We are scoring goals for fun and Fernando Torres is just awesome. His goal reminded me of the way Kenny Dalglish used to finish with that little chip in front of the Kop. The partnership between Torres and Stevie Gerrard is outstanding.'

Benitez was also in confident mood about his team's chances of pushing the likes of Manchester United and Chelsea all the way for domestic glory. He told reporters, 'To score four goals against a tough team is really good and in Fernando Torres we have a player who keeps defenders very busy throughout the game. We are much closer now to the top of the table than we have been in recent years and we have a much better squad. We are scoring a lot of goals and I think we can still improve and get better.'

In the aftermath of that win against Bolton, defender Hyypia had described Torres as 'magnificent' but, as the players prepared for their next match, a return to Reading for a Premier League game just seven weeks or so since Fernando had netted a hat-trick against them in the Carling Cup, Gerrard was even more lavish in his praise of the man with whom he had so quickly formed such a formidable double act.

The comparisons with Rush and Dalglish continued to be made and Gerrard was in no doubt about the qualities of his new team-mate, believing he was one of the most 'frightening strikers in the Premier League'. The England midfield ace said, 'Fernando is getting a lot of praise at the moment and rightly so because the way he has settled into English football has been amazing and the way he has played is frightening. It can be difficult for players from abroad to settle into English football but at the moment Fernando looks like he's been playing here for years. Everyone is talking about the goals he has scored and the way he has scored them but I don't think we should lose sight of all the hard work he is putting in off the ball as well. He defends from the front and doesn't allow defenders to have a second on the ball. If they even think of dwelling on it he is on to them straight away. He is always looking to help the midfielders and the defenders and that makes a big difference.'

One key ingredient Torres had brought to the Liverpool front line was pace. In recent seasons, the most successful Premier League teams had been those whose forwards were blessed with great speed

– the likes of Thierry Henry, Didier Drogba and Cristiano Ronaldo. That was something Liverpool had been lacking but, in Torres, they had a man who could keep up with the best of them and that speed made him a potentially lethal weapon.

Gerrard added, 'Fernando loves running in behind defenders and that gives us the option of hitting him early before defences have even had a chance to react. It is great to have someone who gives us that different option. He's had a great start to his career and long may it continue. I've got to be honest... I'm made up to have him in our team.'

Torres had, of course, served early notice of his abilities with that treble against Reading in late September, but much of the attention following that win and that performance had centred upon the physical treatment that had been dished out to him. Benitez had been critical of the officials on that night, claiming that something needed to be done to protect players like Fernando. But, as he finalised his preparations for the return to the Madejski Stadium, he insisted that he was not tempted to leave his star forward out to keep him safe for future games, not even with Marseille and Manchester United lying in wait.

He said, 'I think it will be difficult for all our players because Reading are physical and they are strong. It is especially difficult for the strikers. But Torres is strong enough and he also has ability and good movement, so if the team is playing well he can manage with the physical game. I think Torres can produce good movement and it will be difficult to control him.'

Sadly for Benitez, his players and the fans, however, the return trip to Berkshire did not go as well as the first had done, as they slumped to a 3–1 defeat, their first loss of the season in the Premier League. But it was not so much the defeat that angered some Liverpool supporters and onlookers as the manner in which Benitez seemed to accept it. Having talked confidently of his side's ability to maintain a title challenge, he then appeared to make a clear statement of where his priorities lay with his substitutions at the Madejski.

With the crucial Champions League tie against Marseille coming up in midweek, he chose to withdraw Torres, Gerrard and Carragher from the fray at Reading. At the time of Torres' substitution, with 30 minutes still remaining, Liverpool were just 2–1 behind. And, almost immediately after Reading had scored their third, Gerrard was replaced.

To those who criticise Benitez for seeming to focus most of his energies on Europe, at the expense of the Premier League, it provided further ammunition with which to castigate him. After all, when trailing in a vital match, what sort of a message is it sending to the fans when you withdraw your three best players in a virtual admission of defeat?

Benitez preferred to focus afterwards on the fact that Reading had been awarded a penalty and his side had had an appeal for one of their own turned down, decisions he felt were crucial in the final outcome. It may be that he had a valid argument, but that still did not change the feelings in some quarters that his ultimate focus lay elsewhere.

He did, though, receive the backing of the local *Daily Post* newspaper. They said of the withdrawal of Gerrard at Reading, 'The decision to substitute Steven Gerrard led to accusations the Spaniard had given up on the game, his team having only moments earlier fallen 3–1 behind to a robust Reading for whom fortune was clearly favouring. But, with a recovery in truth appearing unlikely from a disappointingly subdued Anfield outfit, preserving the skipper was maybe the sensible option.

'Gerrard may have indeed been a driving force in past comebacks, but some are more worthwhile chasing than others. After all, Gerrard had already exerted plenty of energy in making up for the below-par performance from too many of his team-mates on Saturday, continuing his fine goalscoring form with a ninth in ten games to draw Liverpool level in the first half, crashing another shot against the crossbar after the interval and was the visitors' most influential player going forward. The next few days will determine whether Benitez's caution was a wise move.'

Indeed they would. With a trip to the south of France to face Marseille coming just three days after the Reading clash, followed by a home game against Manchester United the following weekend, it was to be a crucial seven days in Liverpool's season.

Having recovered from their horrendous start in the Champions League group stages, Liverpool travelled to France knowing that a win would see them safely through to the knockout phases. And for Fernando, a player who had so longed for top-level European football during his Atletico Madrid days, it was unthinkable that the Reds would now fall at the final hurdle.

He insisted before the game, 'For us, this match is the match of the season so far. Victory or being knocked out will all be decided in 90 minutes. We know we are playing for our future in Europe, but the team is optimistic and I believe we will get through into the knockout rounds.'

And Torres issued a stirring rallying cry ahead of the clash in the Stade Velodrome, urging his team-mates to draw inspiration from the European heroics of Liverpool players in days gone by. He added, 'In the last months, I have looked at some videos of the big historical Liverpool games with the big stars from the club. We need this same spirit to win in Marseille. If we are out of the Champions League, then the players will be the ones to blame. This is evident.

'We all know this match is not easy, but I believe Liverpool will be able to win in France, although it will take a lot of effort. I have always wanted to play in Europe, so if I can score the winner in this game and help get us through then it will be fantastic for me and Liverpool.

'I always dreamed of playing in the Champions League final stages and I want to do that with Liverpool now. Marseille have a little advantage as they are at home, but we want to get revenge for the defeat at Anfield.'

From whatever source it was that Liverpool drew inspiration, draw it they did. They started the game in terrific style and, in truth, it was all over as a contest as early as the 11th minute as quick-fire goals from the dynamic duo of Gerrard and Torres rocked the French side.

They were two early blows from which they never recovered, eventually slumping to a 4–0 defeat as Liverpool added further goals from Dirk Kuyt and Ryan Babel during the second half to complete a stunning victory that would have the whole of Europe sitting up and taking notice. And, if anyone was in any doubt as to Liverpool's determination to again make their mark on a competition in which they had enjoyed so much success in recent seasons, that win rammed home the point.

It was a stunning performance and one that left Benitez rightly delighted. He said, 'I am really proud. It was a fantastic team performance, and that was the key. It was a bad pitch, a windy day but we were compact, worked hard together, were good on the counter-attack and didn't concede. Everything was almost perfect. I say "almost" because we could have scored more goals. You can never be completely perfect, but the team played really well tonight and I can't have any complaints about them.'

There were no complaints from any quarters as Liverpool safeguarded their Champions League place. Mission Improbable, as it had looked after the first three games, had become Mission Accomplished. It was a job very well done.

Now, with Europe on the back burner for a few months, they had to focus all their energies on matters closer to home and the quest for an elusive first Premier League title, starting in the very next game – against Manchester United at Anfield.

5

SO NEAR YET
SO FAR

There are many rivalries in football, but few come close to matching the enmity felt between the supporters of Liverpool and Manchester United. Matches between the two fierce adversaries are those most looked forward to by the respective sets of fans. Their own city derbies against Everton and Manchester City are special fixtures, of that there is no doubt, but it is games between the two old enemies that most get the blood boiling.

It is an intensely bitter rivalry, often unpleasant, and former players have spoken at length of the incredible hatred it generates among those watching from the stands. Liverpool fans had for so long had the bragging rights, pointing to their trophy haul of league titles and European Cups as proof of their superiority, but all that has changed in recent years.

Since the inception of the Premier League, the Reds have failed to finish top of the pile even once, unthinkable really for a club that had previously won 18 League Championship titles. Manchester United, meanwhile, have claimed ten titles since the break-up of the old Football League in 1992/93 as they have dominated the domestic scene under the management of Sir Alex Ferguson.

And they are now closing in on Liverpool's record tally of League Championships, a record of which the Merseysiders are rightly proud. So all the ingredients pointed to a classic encounter at Anfield, one the Reds would be desperate to win, having failed to taste victory on home soil in any of the past five league encounters between the pair – losing four and drawing one.

Liverpool approached the fixture buoyed by that terrific win in Marseille and full of confidence, not least because of the comfort they were drawing from having Torres leading their attacking line.

Fellow striker Dirk Kuyt was certainly impressed with the Spaniard. In the build-up to the United clash, he wrote in his diary on icons.com, 'Torres is the best striker in the league so far this season... Every player has his own ability and his own qualities, but you just try to play your own game. We have four strikers at Liverpool at the moment, but the understanding between us all is really good. I'm very happy Fernando Torres is here because he's a great player who makes a difference in games. He's so quick. He's still young but he's got the ability and technique to pull off moves and score goals.'

All observers, pundits, supporters and team-mates alike had been hugely impressed by the impact Torres had made during the first few months of the season. It seemed he could do no wrong.

Earlier in the campaign, before people had seen the impact he would make and before he had had the chance to properly sample

English football, he had refused to make bold statements about the number of goals he was aiming to score in his debut season. And, for a player whose goals record in Spain was good but not spectacular, that had been deemed fair enough. But now, having already reached double figures, even Fernando himself was beginning to wonder how many he could score and was perhaps reassessing his initial target. His 12 goals at that stage of the season saw him level in second place in the scoring charts with Tottenham's Robbie Keane, behind only Manchester United's Cristiano Ronaldo in the race for the coveted Golden Boot. And he admitted in an interview with the Liverpool website that, while team honours remained his one true goal, individual awards would not go amiss either. He said, 'A team success will always be more important than any individual prize or award, though it is often true that the side which wins the league also has the league's top goalscorer in its team. I have to admit that it would be really nice to finish up as the top goalscorer, but it is more important that Liverpool do really well this season.'

If they were to do well in the championship, games like the one against Manchester United would go a long way to deciding their destiny. The battles between the 'Big Four' are usually closely fought encounters and the side that comes out on top in the majority of those matches has a great chance of being ahead of the pack when the medals are given out in May.

In the build-up to the game, United's assistant manager Carlos Queiroz confessed that he and manager Sir Alex Ferguson were wary of the threat posed by Liverpool, and particularly by Torres. He told the media, 'I have been in England for five years and I have never seen a Liverpool side looking so strong in the league at this point of the season. Torres is doing really well and I am impressed with him. He is already going some way to making the difference for Liverpool this season. I think he's a good finisher and he's a player who gives Liverpool something completely different.

'Certainly we will have to be careful of him because he is dangerous. We are always confident in what we can do and we will not worry too much. But we do recognise his quality.'

Former Anfield star David Fairclough also reckoned Torres could be the difference between the two sides and he was looking to him to inspire Liverpool to a first home victory over their arch rivals for six years. 'I think Torres will give Liverpool a cutting edge over United,' said Fairclough in an interview on liverpoolfc.tv. 'We have lost a couple of league games 1–0 against them in the [recent] past and a big reason for that was not taking our chances early on. You need to take the opportunities when they come along, because against a side like United you won't get a lot of chances. Torres is in such good form and he could make the difference. I expect him to cause the United defence a lot of problems.

'Torres has changed the emphasis of the Liverpool attack. Personally, I felt Liverpool were too predictable last year. Liverpool needed to go out and get something special and I think Torres fits the bill perfectly. He is strong, powerful and direct and that's the type of player that worries defenders.

'There's no reason to think we can't win. United have a lot of great players in their team but at the end of the day we are at home. We should be taking the game to them. I think they would be happy with a draw but we are ready for them, and, if we are able to take the chances when they come along, certainly Liverpool can win.'

Those views from outside the camp were echoed by those within it, with Liverpool's manager and players all looking to Torres to provide the spark they had been lacking in recent meetings with the men from Old Trafford.

Defender Jamie Carragher, who would be looking to stop the likes of Wayne Rooney, Carlos Tevez and Cristiano Ronaldo at one end, while hoping Torres and his striking allies could do the business at the other, also reckoned the Spaniard was the key. He said, 'I hope Fernando is the striker who's going to make the difference for us. He's as good as anyone in Europe at the moment. It's right to compare what he can do for us with what the likes of Tevez and Rooney can do for Manchester United.

'We now have a player in the same bracket, which is great for me as a defender because I know he can get us a goal out of nothing. Fernando is already one of the best players in the Premier League. The way he's been playing he looks unstoppable and I hope that's going to continue. I'm sure there are teams looking at him and saying, "I don't fancy playing against Torres." That's something we've been lacking since Michael Owen left.

'He's certainly looking the part. He's been outstanding since the day he joined. It's not just the goals, it's the all-round work rate. It was a great bit of business by the club to get him here given his age and length of contract for six years.

'I hope we will have him for the peak of his career. We've had a great list of strikers here over the years and, if he keeps going the way he is, he will definitely be up there with the best of them.'

And Carragher was hoping that, finally, with Fernando in the ranks, Liverpool could keep pace with the title challengers for the long haul. 'I'm sure Arsenal, Manchester United and Chelsea will keep winning so it's up to us to prove we can stay with them,' he said. 'It would be really exciting for the Premier League if it's a four-horse race with ten games to go. I hope there are four of us up there come March or April – especially as we're the team which usually falls away. In the past, the consistency of Chelsea was unbelievable and Arsenal went a full season unbeaten. Now the teams in the middle are taking points off us all, making it more competitive. Three points against United would put us right back in it.'

It was interesting that Carragher referred to the signing of Torres as a 'great bit of business' because Benitez chose the build-up to the United game to reveal that it was the desire of the player himself to move to Anfield that clinched the deal ahead of a club willing to pay far more money for him. He told reporters, 'For me, it was just a case of calling him and saying, "We want you to join us." Another top side was making an offer £6m more than us, and we knew how much he was wanted by others. But Torres knew this club and knew that having so many Spanish players and staff would help him a lot.

'When we decided to sign him I knew a lot about his mentality already. I also knew that physically he would be strong enough to play in England. Yes, it was a gamble, but not a big one because of how old he is.'

And the Anfield boss also endorsed the viewpoints of Carragher and Fairclough that the 23-year-old Spaniard could be the missing link as he sought a first Anfield win against United. He added, 'In the past against Manchester United, we have played well and had plenty of the ball, controlling games but without winning them. We know they have good defenders, but also we needed to be stronger in attack. Now, in Fernando Torres, we have someone with pace and ability. And this time, maybe if we have more control of the game, we will be a real threat to them.

'Torres knows all about the United players and will manage that, because he has a lot of experience and a very strong character. I think he could be that extra something which we have needed against United. We are a better squad this season and he is one of the key men in that – and we do have more ways of winning this year.

'It will be difficult, we know that, but I believe that now we have another option that we didn't before. United know he's a good player, they know his quality, and they will be worried about him, that's for sure.'

Worried they may have been, as Queiroz admitted, but the United game was not to have a happy ending for Torres and Liverpool as they crashed to a 1–0 defeat, courtesy of a Carlos Tevez strike shortly before half-time. Although they enjoyed plenty of possession, Liverpool could not turn that into goals, as they lost a league game for the first time that season at Anfield, their second Premier League defeat in a row following that setback at Reading.

It was a crushing blow, made all the more painful by the fact that Tevez's goal was United's only shot on target during the entire 90 minutes. But, while that was of some comfort to Liverpool, Benitez could not hide his disappointment at the setback. He told the media, 'We didn't create that many chances and they didn't have many opportunities either. It's too soon to say we are out of the title race because there is still a long way to go. It will be harder after this game but we have to keep going and think about our next game.'

And that next game was not going to offer too much respite for Liverpool because, just three days after that defeat against United, they travelled south to face another of their main rivals, Chelsea, this time in the Carling Cup. Torres was given the evening off but it was to be another night of disappointment for Reds' fans as their quest for an eighth League Cup triumph came to an end at Stamford Bridge. They were already trailing to a Frank Lampard strike, which took a wicked deflection off Carragher, when Peter Crouch was red-carded for a two-footed lunge on Jon Obi Mikel.

That challenge prompted fury among the Blues' management staff, angry with what they believed was a deliberate attempt by the big striker to injure his opponent. It led to a bitter exchange of views but, for Liverpool, an equally bitter blow was Andrei Shevchenko's 89th-minute goal that condemned them to a second successive defeat for the first time in the season.

In the grand scheme of things, however, a Carling Cup exit was far from the end of the world for Liverpool. With the Premier League, Champions League and FA Cup all still to play for, Benitez was probably mildly relieved to have one less competition on which to focus, particularly one which is almost looked upon as kind of 'consolation prize' these days. What would have concerned him, though, was Liverpool getting back to winning ways immediately following those two defeats. Their next game, however, while not quite on a par with facing Manchester United or Chelsea, promised to be a decent test.

High-flying Portsmouth were the next visitors to Anfield and, after an impressive first half to the season, they had their sights set on a UEFA Cup place and were even being tipped in some quarters to make an unlikely challenge for one of the four available Champions League spots. Having rested several of his main players, including Torres and Gerrard, for the midweek cup trip to Chelsea, Benitez rang the changes again for Pompey's visit and reinstated his big guns into his starting line-up. And it looked as though the rest must have done them good.

Liverpool raced into a two-goal lead inside the first 16 minutes, with Yossi Benayoun opening the scoring and a Sylvain Distin own-goal following quickly to add to the visitors' woes. And Torres made sure of a convincing win with another double after half-time to make the final score 4–1 and put paid to any hopes Portsmouth had of mounting a comeback after Benjani had pulled a goal back.

It was yet another starring performance from the man who was making a habit of being the best player on the pitch. Far from needing time to adapt to the different pace and structure of the English game, he was simply sweeping aside anyone who stood in front of him.

And once more he was the main focus of the post-match headlines. The *Daily Telegraph* stated, 'Old anthem, new star. Those fervent choristers of the famous Kop sang to the man who has stolen their hearts, Fernando Torres. As Liverpool returned to form after recent lapses and Portsmouth's incredible run of six away wins in succession came to an end, even Harry Redknapp was describing him as "a fantastic talent".

'Torres scored twice and was involved in the other two goals and when he was taken off minutes from the end it was to a tumultuous, standing ovation. He is lightning fast, has a vivid imagination and strikes the ball truly. He was the star atop a glittering Liverpool performance that came after recent defeats at home to Manchester United and away to Chelsea.'

Portsmouth boss Redknapp did indeed describe Fernando as a fantastic talent and added, 'He is a top striker who is at another level. He is in a top-four team with a lot of good players who can tear you apart on the day. Make no mistake, Liverpool can beat anybody on their day.'

That brace against Portsmouth took his tally for Liverpool to 15 goals in just 22 games for the club, with nine of those goals coming in the Premier League. That strike rate made for an interesting comparison with the last big-name striker to join Liverpool from Spanish football, Fernando Morientes. The former Real Madrid star arrived at Anfield with a huge reputation and was one of the most feared forwards in European football, but he struggled badly in his season-and-a-half in English football. And, despite his physical stature – he stands 6ft 1in and weighs 12-and-a-half stone – and his undoubted aerial threat, Benitez believes one of the reasons for Morientes' relative failure was his inability to stand up to the rigours of the Premier League.

The Liverpool manager admitted, 'When we signed Morientes, his mentality was really good. I was looking for a player good in the air and a target man. But Morientes couldn't handle it physically. Torres can. He is quick and strong. And he's younger.'

And Benitez also reckoned there were a couple of other factors working in Fernando's favour. He added, 'He is a Spanish player who has come to a team with a Spanish manager and some Spanish-speaking team-mates. It can be difficult for a manager to explain what he wants, but I tell him in Spanish and can explain things that maybe others couldn't. It is not the same to go through a translator.

'Torres will get better because he wants to improve. His mentality is good. If you tell him he needs to work hard, he works harder. If you need him to stay and practise after training, he stays and practises.'

And it was clear that all that hard work and practice was paying off. But neither Fernando nor his Liverpool team-mates could afford to relax. That win against Portsmouth was the first of what they hoped would be four out of four over the busy Christmas period, which would be sure to be a real test of Torres' stamina as he was more used to having a winter break during his days in La Liga.

Although it had been an encouraging first half to the season for Liverpool, they still found themselves outside the top four, lying in fifth place, a point behind Chelsea and Manchester City. Fourth, though, was merely the limit of their ambitions. They had their eyes on the ultimate prize, the Premier League trophy. But a glance at the top of the table made for worrying viewing for the Anfield faithful as they saw their side trailing leaders Arsenal by a massive ten points. Manchester United, who were lying in second place going into the festive period, could also boast a not insubstantial six-point advantage over their north-west rivals.

So, with ground to be made up on the leaders, Liverpool would not have been too disappointed to be handed a Boxing Day trip to rock-bottom Derby, who had only one win to their name four-and-a-half months into the season. In the end, however, Benitez will have been happy to see his side come away having narrowly scraped all three points.

Torres gave them the perfect start at Pride Park with an 11th-minute goal to open the scoring, but they needed a scrappy last-minute winner from Gerrard to make the points safe after Jay McEveley's second-half goal had looked for a long time like earning the hosts an unlikely share of the spoils.

It was a poor performance, but all that really mattered for Liverpool was that they got the win they needed to keep them in touch with the Premier League's pace-setters. Once more it was Torres and Gerrard who produced the goods when it mattered to win the game and that dynamic duo had now netted 16 of Liverpool's 33 league goals for the campaign.

And Ryan Babel, third in that goalscoring list but with only three goals to his name, called on his team-mates to help ease the burden on their two star performers. He said on the club's website, 'I think you can expect those types of performances from Torres and Gerrard, but they also need us to help them. If they do all the work they can't develop things for the team. So all our players have to work hard so those players can give something extra. They can give something extra because I think they have already been playing at the highest level for a couple of years in Spain and in the Premier League.

'If we hadn't won at Derby I think people would have asked themselves, "Are Liverpool really strong enough for the title?" We made it difficult for ourselves because we wanted an early goal, which we got, but then had enough chances to score a second. We failed and they came level and it was more difficult than when we were in front. But we did win, we got the three points and we have to look forward now to the next game against Manchester City.'

Looking forward to the game against City they may have been, but Liverpool will have been far from happy at the outcome of that match, struggling to a 0–0 draw at the City of Manchester Stadium against the side they had leapfrogged to claim fourth place following that victory at Derby.

Interestingly, it was only the third time in 15 games they had played together that neither Torres nor Gerrard had scored, seeming to back up Babel's point that the others at Anfield needed to weigh in to take the pressure off the Reds' superstars. The question seemed to be: if Torres and Gerrard didn't perform to their best, who would step up to the plate to drag the team to victory?

It all made for a frustrating end to the year for Liverpool, and unfortunately for them the new one didn't start any better as they began 2008 with a draw at home to Wigan, a game they would surely have expected to win and the sort of fixture they so obviously needed to win if they were to achieve their aim of title glory.

The likes of Manchester United and Chelsea had developed a habit of finding a way to win against opposition from the lower reaches of the league, even when not playing well, and it was a habit Liverpool desperately needed to pick up.

As it was, another fantastic Torres goal was not enough to claim all three points, as Wigan hit back with a stunning equaliser with just ten minutes remaining from the most unlikely of sources, central defender Titus Bramble.

It was a further setback for Liverpool in their quest to close the gap on the leaders, but Benitez refused to be downhearted. He told the media, 'You have to try to play one game at a time if you can, because if you think about the gap you will play with more pressure. We need to play well, create chances and score goals, then see every week what the situation is.

'For sure, it's more difficult now, especially when you know you are creating chances in all of the games but cannot score that second goal and kill the game. I can say a lot of things but at the end of the day you need to win if you are to reduce the gap. It's not a time for talking, it's a time to play well, score goals and win games.'

Easier said than done of course, but, while Benitez was issuing all the right messages and rallying calls in public, in private he must have been concerned about his side's inability to kill off games and their seeming over-reliance on Gerrard and Torres to score their goals.

Perhaps a break from league action was exactly what was called for at this stage, although if Benitez's mood was darkening it won't have been helped by a 1–1 draw at League One strugglers Luton in the third round of the FA Cup. On the verge of administration and beset with financial problems, events off the pitch at Luton had overshadowed the build-up to the game. For them, a draw and a replay at Anfield, ensuring a healthy share of bumper gate receipts, was arguably the best result they could have imagined.

For Liverpool, however, it was another match they could do without. But an unconvincing display at Kenilworth Road meant they had only themselves to blame for finding another fixture added to their calendar. As it was, by the time that replay came around just ten days later, Luton had gone into administration, sold two of their best players and their manager Kevin Blackwell had served notice of his intention to resign.

So it can have come as no surprise that a strong Liverpool side, with Torres included in the starting line-up for his first taste of the FA Cup, having been rested for the first meeting, ran out comfortable 5–0 winners.

But, while that win gave Liverpool supporters something to cheer, their Premier League form was still giving cause for concern. In between those two cup ties against Luton, they slipped to a third successive league draw, this time at Middlesbrough, where again only a stunning strike from Torres saved them from defeat.

They were now 12 points behind leaders Arsenal and Manchester United and, with only 16 games of the Premier League season remaining, that was a significant gap to try to bridge. And the fans, it appeared, were beginning to get restless.

James Carroll, from fans' website shanklygates.co.uk, told the *Observer*, 'The first half [against Middlesbrough] was the worst we've played all season. If I was a Boro fan, I'd be gutted not to have won. They outfought us and that's not nice to see. We seemed to have no passion and were just launching it forward.

'Babel was on for the second half and I thought we'd really give it a go, but we didn't. They hit the post and it was only when Torres scored we looked interested. His goal was brilliant, but we've said before we are over-reliant on some individual players and the way we played it looked like they had more than us.'

And it was becoming clear that events off the pitch were starting to affect matters on it. For all that the players insisted they concentrated only on the football, the very public spat that was taking place between Benitez and the club's American owners, George Gillett and Tom Hicks, over the direction of the club was obviously taking its toll.

Defensive stalwart Sami Hyypia said as much after the draw with Middlesbrough when he told reporters, 'We seem to be becoming like Newcastle. Every time we pick up a paper, there seems to be something new. But our job is to concentrate on the games. In the football world there are some things that happen very quickly and you can't do anything about them. The players hope that, if there are arguments, they can be sorted out.'

It was against this unsettled backdrop that the players had to plan for their next challenge, a Premier League match at home to Aston Villa. And ahead of that game against Martin O'Neill's men, Liverpool's players were once again forced to admit that it was time others stepped up to share the burden of carrying the team's goalscoring hopes with Torres.

Dutch striker Dirk Kuyt said, 'We can't keep relying on Torres. He is having an unbelievable season, especially as he's come in from a foreign country and does not speak English very well.

He's one of the best in Europe at the moment and frightening for defenders.'

John Arne Riise agreed with his team-mate's assessment and also called for others to step up to the mark. He told liverpoolfc.tv, 'People talk about Torres and Gerrard scoring all our goals, so we need others to come in and do that. Now it's up to wingers, midfielders and even defenders to share the goals because Torres can't win every game.'

Two others did step up to aid the cause against Villa with Yossi Benayoun and Peter Crouch getting the goals in a 2–2 draw. The match, however, was only half the story.

The game was played out against an incredible backdrop of protest and vitriol from the Liverpool fans, relishing the first opportunity to vent their collective spleen against Gillett and Hicks. If there was indeed a power struggle going on between the club's manager and their owners, it was clear where the Anfield faithful's loyalties lay.

By now it had become public knowledge that Liverpool had sounded out Jurgen Klinsmann back in November about the possibility of his succeeding Benitez in the Anfield hot-seat. That revelation was met with widespread scorn in the red half of Merseyside and the fans let their feelings be known in incredibly vocal fashion, calling for the Americans to relinquish their ownership of the club.

Unsurprisingly then, the game became almost a secondary concern, but what would have been of primary concern for Liverpool's players – irrespective of what was happening behind the scenes – was the alarming slump in their form that was threatening to derail their season. Certainly, it may already have caused fatal damage to their hopes of being in the title shake-up come the end of the season as they languished a whopping 14 points behind the top two of Manchester United and Arsenal.

Crouch admitted to journalists after the Villa draw, 'I think when we started this season we all felt that we were going to mount a serious challenge but that doesn't seem to be the case at the minute. We've fallen way behind and it isn't good enough. I think there's enough talent in the dressing room [to be challenging at the top].

'We've got a good squad of players. Whether it's good enough to win the title I don't know, but it's certainly good enough to be in a better position than the one we're in. As players, we have to look to cement that Champions League spot for next year. I think that's the minimum and anything upwards of that is what we've got to strive for.'

Next up was what should have been a routine FA Cup fourth-round romp at Anfield against non-league Havant & Waterlooville. The final 5–2 scoreline suggests that was exactly what it was, but that does not tell the tale of how Liverpool twice had to come from behind to defeat the plucky part-timers.

Ultimately, there was no harm done and Liverpool's discomfort was simply a bit of a laugh for the neutrals who were firmly in the minnows' corner, especially after they opened the scoring and then added a second to make the score 2–1 at one stage. But it was no laughing matter for those within Anfield and the convincing look of the final score could not hide the fact that clearly all was not well at the club, either on or off the pitch.

Further proof, if it were needed, came in the very next game when they travelled south to London to take on West Ham at Upton Park and left empty-handed following a 1–0 defeat. It was another crushing blow to what were by now becoming forlorn hopes of lasting the pace in the title race. Indeed, some would argue that, other than during their blistering start in the first few weeks of the season, they were never even in the race.

And, in fact, they were now in a real battle with Everton, Aston Villa and Manchester City for fourth place. Failure to secure that, and the Champions League football that went with it, was unthinkable, particularly with the volatile boardroom war that was being fought behind the scenes.

BBC Radio Merseyside journalist Gary Flintoff was arguably speaking for half a city when he said after the defeat at Upton Park, 'This game for me sums up Liverpool's season in many ways. They did much better in the second half and yet right at the end they have piled everyone forward for a corner, and yet conspired to leave themselves open on the counter-attack and lose the game.

'It was tough on Jamie Carragher to concede the penalty [which Mark Noble converted] because he was one of the better players. Liverpool have the chance to get back to form against Sunderland on Saturday but they face a real challenge now for fourth place.'

Liverpool had now gone five games without a Premier League win, more like relegation form than that of a side with pretensions to be crowned champions. And there was much relief when they triumphed 3–0 in their next game against Roy Keane's Sunderland.

The match was a rare opportunity for Torres to start alongside

Crouch in attack, and the pair did well together, each scoring a goal. It will come as no surprise that Liverpool's third was netted by Gerrard.

It was a much-needed three points and a relieved Benitez admitted in his press conference afterwards, 'I think it was important to score the first goal and win the game and 3–0 is a fantastic result. I must also thank our supporters because they were behind the team. We needed to be patient and they were with us. As soon as we scored the first goal, you could see the celebrations and everyone was pulling together.'

Liverpool were hoping this result would see them turn the corner and one former Anfield legend reckoned Benitez should stick with the Torres–Crouch pairing up front to give his side the best chance of success. Ian Rush said, 'There's no doubt that they're the most in-form pairing at present, so I think now is the time to see if they can develop into a decent strike force. The match against Sunderland was only the third time they've started a match together in the Premier League, and there were one or two signs that they could flourish. But the fact is we will never know unless we give them a chance to gel.'

And the former Anfield sharp-shooter believed Crouch's aerial ability could create the opportunities for Torres to increase his goal output still further. 'I've said before that Peter Crouch has done nothing wrong this season, and with three goals in his last three appearances he's flying. But his presence can also help Fernando Torres,' continued Rush on the Liverpool website. 'By virtue of his height alone, he occupies one or two defenders, giving Torres more room to operate in, and he showed with the flick-on that created Torres' goal that he can be very much a traditional target man. In situations like that, it's important that one player is able to anticipate the flick-ons of the other, but Torres is a very intelligent striker and that will never be a problem to a player of his class.'

Before Rush could get his wish to see Torres and Crouch paired in attack again, however, Benitez had to suffer the anxious wait all top managers go through every time their players go away on international duty with their countries. There is always the risk they will come back injured or carrying knocks and the Spaniard's worst fears were realised when Torres reported back to the club's Melwood training ground suffering from a thigh injury.

He sustained the injury just 23 minutes into Spain's friendly clash against France, forcing him out of the action, and he told the Spanish press afterwards, 'I preferred not to risk it. I demanded the change.' So it was his decision to go off against the French in a bid to safeguard his participation in Liverpool's next match, a crucial game away to Chelsea.

But, although Fernando had done the sensible thing in getting off the pitch as soon as he felt a twinge, and with the Spanish management suggesting that the injury was not a serious one, Benitez could not hide his frustration at seeing his plans disrupted. He moaned, 'This is why I am so frustrated about international friendly matches being played at such an important time in the season. We will have to wait and see how bad the problem is for Torres but he is a doubt for Sunday [against Chelsea]. We cannot change anything now so we will use the players who are fit and available.'

In the end, the optimism of Fernando and the Spanish national team's medical staff proved misplaced as he was forced to sit out the game at Stamford Bridge. With Chelsea also missing their star striker, Didier Drogba, perhaps the absences were evened out, but, once it was confirmed that Torres would miss the trip to west London, Benitez was quick to again voice his displeasure at the situation. He told the media, 'The news on Torres is that it is a hamstring injury. Normally it is a week when a player goes off like this. It is a big problem for us. We have three big games in ten days in three different competitions, and we have lost our top goalscorer. It is difficult to be calm about it... this was another international friendly in a busy period for clubs at this time of the season.

'It is crazy enough they go away and have different training systems, diets, new ideas. And then they get injured. We have got some confidence back with a 3–0 win over Sunderland and a very good second-half performance. But then a lot of players are away all over the world and we are left to train with just a few, it makes things very difficult.

'It is hard to see who is to blame for Torres' injury. But the authorities are talking of changing the schedule and to pay money if you lose players. But it is not about money. We are playing at Chelsea fighting for fourth position, then we have Barnsley in the FA Cup and after that Inter Milan in the Champions League. That is three important competitions, and if you lose someone like Torres, who was scoring lots of goals, it is a big, big loss. You can always blame someone, but any solution would be better than this. Every time we have an international break we are talking of a solution and a way to improve things, but still nothing happens.

'The players go off with different coaches, some have to train hard and some have to learn a different system. The training can be too intense and people get injured. It would be better to play all the internationals at the same time, maybe at the end of the season rather than keep sending the players all around the world.'

Perhaps it was the absence of Torres and Drogba that contributed to the stalemate at Stamford Bridge as the two sides had to settle for a point apiece in a 0–0 draw. For Liverpool, it was a fifth draw in seven Premier League games but this counted as a far better point than some of the previous ones had done.

Benitez chose not to risk Torres for the next game, an FA Cup fifth-round tie at home to Barnsley, and it was a decision he perhaps came to regret after the mighty Merseysiders were humbled by their far less illustrious opponents, losing 2–1 to a side fighting a relegation battle in the Championship. But the manager had opted to protect his star striker for the bigger challenges that lay ahead, starting with the resumption of the Champions League and a last-16 meeting with Inter Milan.

After they had confirmed their place in the knockout stages with that win in Marseille in December, Torres had spoken of his desire to meet Real Madrid in the sudden-death round. But, rather than the Spanish super-power, it was an Italian one that stood in Liverpool's way.

But no matter that the opponents were not his former city rivals, on the eve of the Anfield clash against Inter, Torres could not hide his excitement at having the chance to qualify for the latter stages of Europe's premier competition. He told the reporters ahead of the game, 'This is a very big game for the fans and for us. I came here to play in this type of game, in the Champions League and in other competitions. Inter Milan are a very good team but I think we can beat them. Why not?'

Liverpool had, of course, enjoyed a fantastic recent record in the competition, winning it in 2005 and finishing runners-up in 2007. Add that to their success in the old European Cup in the 1970s and 1980s and Fernando was only too aware what the tournament meant to the club. 'Reaching two Champions League finals in three years is an incredible achievement,' he continued. 'It takes something special to do that and you don't do that unless you have a very good manager. That is another reason why I came to Liverpool, to work with the manager, and I have learned a lot from him since I joined.

'We have an opportunity to get an important win. The supporters, the players, the staff at Liverpool are like a big family. It is a different mentality to most other clubs and we need to play like a team.

'Big teams win the important games and we are a big team. After losing to Marseille at home, we knew we had to beat Porto at home and then win in Marseille and in both games we played really, really well. We scored four goals against Porto and four against Marseille. This is what Liverpool can do and we need to do it again in a big game against Inter Milan.

'We were third in our group, we needed to win our remaining games and we did. I also saw Liverpool beat Barcelona in the Champions League last season. That was also a big game, Liverpool played very, very well and got a great result. To win 2–1 away at Barcelona is a big result. They [Barcelona] were the best team in the world when it comes to ability because they have so many great players but Liverpool played like a team and if you play like a team you can win every game against every team. If we play like a team [against Inter] then we can win, for sure.'

And win they did on a night that turned out to be every bit as good as Torres had hoped it would. Although they were made to work hard for the win, and had to wait until late in the day to secure it, two goals in the last five minutes from Dirk Kuyt and Steven Gerrard meant they would to travel to Milan for the return leg a fortnight later with a comfortable 2–0 lead to protect.

It was a vintage performance from Liverpool as they claimed their 100th European win on home soil and Benitez was delighted. He said, 'We knew that it could come late and to score two goals was fantastic. In the end it was perfect because a clean sheet and two goals will mean it will be difficult for them, but also they are a very good team so we must be careful.'

It was a vital win for Liverpool after a difficult few weeks, particularly after losing to Barnsley in the FA Cup, and Benitez added, 'I think everyone knew we needed this. It was really important for the club and fans that we won. I have always had confidence in this team and we will win a lot of games.

'The determination to prove people wrong was no different to any other game. We have not had much luck of late and the confidence is low but we must keep working hard and that is what we did.'

What was important for Liverpool now was that they backed up that win with an upsurge in their Premier League form. And they wasted no time in doing that in their next match at home to Middlesbrough. And what a game it was for Torres, who netted another hat-trick in the 3–2 win, his second of the season and his first at Anfield. It took his tally for the season against Boro to four after his stunning strike at the Riverside earlier in the season and the Teessiders must have been glad they wouldn't have to face him again for the remainder of the campaign.

Certainly, Gareth Southgate must have been sick of the sight of him. Having said that, he'd already pretty much had enough of him from a previous encounter three years previously when the Middlesbrough boss was still a Middlesbrough defender. Boro met Atletico Madrid in a pre-season friendly and Southgate recalled, 'You could see the talent he had even then and how he'd fit into the English game without any problems. I must say I didn't do particularly well – I did retire for a reason! He's one of the outstanding players in this league and gives them [Liverpool] something that, when he's been injured, they haven't had. His movement is so good, even though we gifted him two of his goals.'

His second treble of the campaign took his overall tally past the 20 mark in another blistering display that left Benitez once again extolling his striker's virtues. He said, 'I was really happy with the performance. I think coming after a Champions League game the most important thing was to win. After we scored the third goal on the counter-attack, you could see that we could score more, but they put us under a bit of pressure because they have some good players in attack. It's always difficult to score more than 20 goals, but Torres has done it in his first season. We knew that he was a player with power and pace. He can kill defenders.

'This year, 21 goals is a very good figure, but he can improve. He will get goals every year because he is always ready. He has the pace, ambition and ability but he can improve his finishing and control. There are some things he is doing well and can do better.

'We spoke this week about things he needs to work on in training sessions and he is committed and ready to do that. He is a good learner and wants to improve. Fernando is a player with big ambition. He wants to progress, to score goals and to be one of the best. He is learning the killer instinct of a striker and it is very positive.

'In some games early on he missed some chances, but with each game he is improving. He is still young and can get better. When he was at Atletico, he was the key player for six or seven years. He was the captain, the icon of the club, so he knows how to deal and manage with pressure.'

Fernando himself was naturally delighted with his second hat-trick of the season but revealed to the media afterwards that he would happily swap personal success in front of goal for overall team glory. 'Maybe people will look at it as a successful season for me, but I'll only consider the season a success if we win something,' he said. 'I'm 23 and I've never won a real medal. The only time was when I was an Under-16 and Under-19 player and that's a long time ago. I've come here to win titles and whether that's this season, next season, I don't know when, but that's my target. I hope I'm here for a long time, I want to stay here for a long time. I have six years on my contract and if everything is OK maybe it will be more.

'I'd prefer to be remembered as someone who helped Liverpool to win trophies than a great goalscorer. I'm here to win titles. The Champions League is a very important target for me. I've got to score goals because it's my job but it's not the most important thing for me.'

His three goals against Boro also meant he had now scored 15 Premier League goals and was well on course to become the first Liverpool player since Robbie Fowler in 1995/96 to score 20 league goals in a season. 'It's the second hat-trick of my Liverpool career so it was a very happy day for me,' he added. 'It was fantastic to score a hat-trick in front of the Kop. It was my first at Anfield and I feel very comfortable playing here.

'When I played in Madrid, I watched Premier League games a lot and knew it would be difficult to play here and that the defenders are very strong so I would have to say it's a surprise to have scored this many goals so quickly.

'Twenty-one goals is my best season yet and we still have a maximum of 18 games to go, in the Premier League and Champions League, so hopefully I can score more. I'm happy when the team wins, but I'm not thinking about scoring 30.

'I didn't set myself a target at the start of the season. Obviously, I want to score as many goals as I can, it's my job, but whether it's 20, 25, I've no target. I just want to score as many goals as I can to make sure Liverpool are a success. It's not about me, it's about the team.'

Fernando was also quick to pay tribute to the part Rafael Benitez and his team-mates had played in his success since his arrival in England. He said, 'You cannot score three goals in a game without the help of your manager and your team-mates, so I would like to thank them. The manager signed me for Liverpool so I am really grateful for that, and he also works with me all the time trying to improve me and make me a better player. I think my game has already improved and will continue to improve under Rafa Benitez. The most important thing is that the team is successful, that is the only thing that matters.

'Everyone at the club has to focus on trying to finish in the top four so the win against Middlesbrough was a very important result for us.'

Torres' latest hat-trick also kept him on course for an extremely noteworthy distinction, as his 21 goals in his first 31 games put him in line to have the most prolific debut season of any striker in Liverpool's modern history.

His goals were coming at a rate of one every 1.48 games which compared favourably when ranked alongside some other Anfield greats. Their stats for their first full seasons in the famous all-red strip read: John Aldridge (a goal every 1.55 games), Ian Rush (1.63), Roger Hunt (1.65), Robbie Fowler (1.83), Michael Owen (1.91) and Kenny Dalglish (2). It was exalted company to be in at all, let alone to be leading.

But, although that was a very significant achievement, so far at least, Torres had a little way to go before he could justifiably claim to be the Premier League's deadliest marksman. His 15 League goals had come in 1,775 minutes of playing time – a goal every 118 minutes. Impressive shooting it must be said, but it left him only third in the list for the season so far, behind Cristiano Ronaldo (a goal every 92 minutes) and Emmanuel Adebayor (one every 113 minutes). But it did mean he was some way ahead of some of the game's other leading strikers, including Yakubu (a goal every 133 minutes), Robbie Keane (one every 152 minutes), Didier Drogba (one every 177 minutes) and Wayne Rooney (one every 183 minutes).

So it was not surprising that he was full of confidence as Liverpool looked to back up that impressive win against Middlesbrough by continuing their Premier League recovery away to Bolton in their next game. It would also be fair to say that the Reebok Stadium had not been a happy hunting ground for the Reds in recent memory. In fact, Rafa Benitez had failed to register a win in any of his three previous visits there as Liverpool manager and it was a fixture he and his side, if they were honest, probably did not relish.

But with Torres in such hot form, maybe this would be the year for Benitez and his boys to end their Bolton jinx. Certainly Dirk Kuyt was optimistic about their chances of finally laying that ghost to rest, especially with his Spanish strike partner banging in goals from all angles. Kuyt said, 'It was very important to get the win against Middlesbrough because we still want to do something in the league and we definitely want to play in the Champions League next season. We did our job and got the three points and now we have to get as many points as we can from the league games we have coming up.

'We didn't make a good start in that game but, having beaten Inter Milan a few days before, we had the confidence to go and turn it around. Fernando got us back into it and from then on we went on to control things, even though we had a bit of a scare late on.

'I was happy with the two wins we had against Inter Milan and

Middlesbrough and now we have to look to get another one against Bolton. We are in the middle of a run of four league games before we play Inter again and we have to try and do everything we can to make the most of those games and get ourselves into fourth position.

'Hopefully, we will get three more wins because that is exactly what we need. We showed against Inter that we can beat anyone but we have to be focused on this game [against Bolton].'

Kuyt had spoken before about his admiration for Torres but, as the season wore on, he was growing even more impressed with his young colleague who he rated as one of the most exciting strikers in European football. 'He is unbelievable, a really good player,' the Dutchman said. 'I have never seen someone who is that quick with the ball. I don't think anyone is as quick as Fernando is with the ball at his feet. He showed it again against Middlesbrough and if you have a player like that in your team you have to be really happy. He is definitely going to get better as well because he is still very young and he has only been playing football in this country for just over six months.

'No disrespect to Atletico Madrid but I think Liverpool is the real thing, a really big club, one of the biggest in Europe and with the kind of players he has behind him here – the likes of Steven Gerrard, Javier Mascherano and Xabi Alonso – he is only going to improve. It is great for everyone in the team to have a player like Fernando up front because he is unbelievable. I think he played really well against Inter but he was even better against Boro. The hat-trick he scored against them was his second of the season already so that is really good for him and for us.'

And Kuyt will certainly have been hoping that Torres could continue his fine form against a Bolton side that was battling at the other end of the table. But, while being wary of the threat posed by the Spaniard, Trotters' defender Matt Taylor insisted his team would not be taking any particular measures to nullify him. 'There are no special plans for Torres, we'll have to shackle him but we won't change our game for him,' Taylor told setantasports.com. 'There are plenty of fantastic players in the Premier League, arguably the best players play here, so we'll have no special plans and we've just got to make sure we get our own game right.

'It's a big game, but we tend to respond well in big games – just before I arrived [from Portsmouth in the January transfer window] the lads beat Manchester United at home. It's always tough against Liverpool but there's no reason why we can't get a result.'

On the day, though, it was Liverpool that got the result and, although Bolton succeeded in their aim of keeping Torres off the score sheet, goals from Ryan Babel and Fabio Aurelio, to add to Jussi Jasskelainen's early own-goal, ensured that the visitors left with all three points following a 3–1 win.

That victory was a decisive statement of Liverpool's intent, coming as it did against opponents they had struggled to overcome in recent times. With the battle for fourth place intensifying with Everton, Manchester City and Aston Villa all pushing Liverpool hard for that crucial last Champions League spot, this was a clear signal that the Reds would not be giving up that coveted European place without an almighty scrap.

And if people weren't convinced after back-to-back wins against tricky opponents in Middlesbrough and Bolton, then Liverpool's next match surely silenced the doubters who were predicting that their mid-season wobble could prove costly. The Reds were simply in irresistible form as they swept West Ham aside 4–0 at Anfield, with Torres helping himself to his third hat-trick of the season, and his second in successive games on home soil. It was a breathtaking display of finishing at the very highest level.

The *Liverpool Echo* described his performance by saying, 'That's 24 goals in just 33 games for Torres. His treble brought Anfield to its feet and the ovation Torres was afforded as he left the scene of his triumph was a fitting tribute to a player who is every inch the archetypal Liverpool hero. Fearless, energetic, combative and inspirational, Torres already ranks alongside even Steven Gerrard and Jamie Carragher in the affections of the Kop – and he has only been here for seven months.'

Rafael Benitez was, understandably, equally delighted with his main marksman. He told the media, 'To score hat-tricks in consecutive home games is a fantastic achievement and everyone at the club is very proud of that. Fernando is on fire at the moment. We are playing with a lot of confidence now.

'We started the season well, but at this crucial stage of the season we are playing really well and you can see the team operating as a team... that is really important. We have three more points and we are closer now, it depends on us. If we can beat Newcastle we will approach the Inter game with a lot of confidence.'

Unsurprisingly, it was Gerrard who scored the fourth goal to complete the rout of the Hammers and he led the tributes from inside the dressing room to the man with whom he had formed such a lethal partnership. 'Fernando is frightening,' insisted the Liverpool skipper. 'From the opening home game of the season against Chelsea when he scored a cracker, he has been consistent all the way. He got off to a good start then and now he has hit 18 Premier League goals, the first person to do that here since Michael Owen. So far so good and hopefully he can continue like this right to the end of the season.

'He has pace, power and is very direct but the most important thing for us is his work rate. He hasn't come here as a star, he is chipping in with his work as well and when you get that from a player as well you cannot ask for much more.'

His hat-trick against the east Londoners also meant another personal landmark for Torres as he became the first Liverpool player for almost 60 years, since Jackie Balmer in November 1946, to score successive hat-tricks in home games for the club. He said, 'I only learned of the record after the game and it is a big honour for me. This club has a wonderful history so to be a part of that is very special and it is something I am very proud of. But it is also a record for everyone at the club because it would be impossible for me to score goals if it was not for my team-mates, the manager, the coaching staff, everyone.'

Torres had, in his short space of time at Anfield, achieved hero-like status and the supporters almost took the roof off Anfield with the ovation he received when he was substituted minutes after completing his hat-trick against the Hammers. It was a reception that took even him by surprise. 'It was incredible,' he added. 'The roar from the crowd was fantastic and it made the hairs stand up on the back of my neck. I feel really lucky and also humble to be loved by the crowd but what I would say is that I love them also. They have supported me since I first came to the club and I want to keep on scoring goals for them. The Liverpool fans are special and it is an honour for me to play for them, so if I can make them happy then I will be happy.'

Everyone at Anfield, it seemed, was happy with Torres. And his team-mates were backing him to continue to improve on his goalscoring form and book himself a place in the record books as the Premier League's most successful foreign debutant ever.

His three goals against West Ham had taken his tally for the season to 24, 18 of which had come in the Premier League, meaning he was just six goals short of the 24 that former Manchester United striker Ruud van Nistelrooy scored in his first season in England. Strike partner Kuyt insisted, 'He's on his way to the very top, if he's not there already. It's a big achievement for him if he can reach 20 league goals, especially in his first season, and it's unbelievable how quickly he has settled in at Liverpool because I know what it is like to try and settle in here. It's especially hard when you're from Spain and you speak a different language, so to play so well in his first season is amazing. He can only be proud of what he's done. He could score 30 goals this season. If we can keep playing like this as a team, we know we can give the chances to Fernando.

'At the moment, he's scoring nearly every game and, if he keeps doing that, we are going to make fourth easily. But we'll have to see what happens. It looks really easy what he does, but it isn't that easy.

It's because he's a great player and he's doing really well. It's just his first season and he can only get better and better. He's unbelievable. It's a little bit boring to say it all the time because he seems to score hat-tricks every week almost!'

Next up for Liverpool were Newcastle, meaning a return to Anfield for Michael Owen, who himself once occupied the position now being filled by Torres as the goalscoring darling of the Kop. Owen had been linked with a return to Liverpool when he left Real Madrid at the start of the 2005/06 season and, on the eve of the Magpies' visit to Anfield, Rafael Benitez revealed that he also considered making a move for the striker before the start of the current campaign. He was quick to stress, however, that Torres had always been his number-one target. Benitez said, 'In the summer, Michael was one of the names on the list of strikers we were pursuing, but Fernando was always top of that list, and the one we wanted above all others. When you talk to Steven Gerrard and Jamie Carragher they say what a great player Michael is, and they wanted him, because he is a great finisher and a good striker. But Torres was our top choice because he was young, because he is very quick and he has such potential. He had all the conditions we wanted, and we are very, very happy with our decision.

'When Michael is fit he is one of the best forwards in the world. But we thought that maybe Nando was younger, quicker and could do what we wanted, which was to run behind defenders from deeper, and play for the team. It was not just my decision to buy Fernando... the scouting department were looking at a lot of strikers. They saw the pace and ability and hunger of Torres. Michael is great but we are happy that Torres is here. He has so much potential, and he is still learning. He knows he can improve, he knows he must get better, but the good thing is he is such a nice lad, so down-to-earth, and he wants to improve and get better.

'He was the main player at Atletico, but he doesn't want to be the superstar. He is humble and he has a lot of good people around him – his family, his girlfriend – who all have good ideas about his future.'

Torres' attempt to become the first Liverpool player in history to score three hat-tricks in a row at home came to an end against Newcastle, but he was on target once more, scoring the second goal in a 3–0 win, with the others coming from Jermaine Pennant and Steven Gerrard to keep the Liverpool bandwagon rolling forward.

Benitez said afterwards, 'We needed to win and we scored three goals and kept another clean sheet. We were also able to rest some players as well so it was perfect. Both Torres and Gerrard are playing well and that is important for us. If they have the space, with the quality and pace they have, they can kill defenders.'

His opposite number, former Anfield legend Kevin Keegan, also singled out Liverpool's dynamic duo for praise. He said, 'You are only seeing the start of it at the moment, but what you are seeing if you are Rafa Benitez or a Liverpool fan is something that makes you go "wow". It's not what it is now but what it could be in the future that must frighten teams.

'Liverpool have the players who can really hurt you and, in Gerrard and Torres, they certainly had that. They are building a good partnership, realising the strengths of each other, and they are exploiting that on the pitch. The partnership between Gerrard and Torres is a combination that can only get better.'

With ten goals between them in the last five games, it was impossible to argue with that sentiment and Fernando was loving every minute of it. He said, 'When you play alongside a player like Stevie, it is easy to score like I have been. I am very comfortable with the partnership I have with Stevie and he is comfortable with me. We now must play like this for a long time together. We know where each other is running, where we are. I score, Stevie scores, and the team is winning. That is the most important thing. We both do our jobs and the team is winning. That is all we are trying to do.'

Victory over Newcastle was the perfect confidence boost as Liverpool prepared to travel to Italy for the second leg of their Champions League last-16 clash against Inter Milan. Leading 2–0 from the first meeting two weeks earlier, the Reds were firmly in the driving seat but knew they could take nothing for granted against the reigning Serie A champions.

Fernando said, 'We can look to the Inter Milan game with confidence. It is a very important game for us, and we must keep this form going. We are confident of progressing in the competition in the San Siro. We had an excellent victory against Inter at Anfield, and we know if we score one goal in Milan it makes it very difficult for them, already 2–0 behind.

'They are one of the best teams in Europe at the moment, but we are confident. We expect to play deep and try for the counter-attack and, although we know Inter are a good team, the first goal is very important. If we score first it will be difficult for them to score four times.'

Manager Benitez was also approaching the game in confident

mood, especially as his star duo of Gerrard and Torres were displaying the sort of form that made them the envy of just about every leading manager in Europe. And Benitez reckoned the arrival of the Spanish ace in the summer had brought an extra dimension to Gerrard's game and made him an even better player. The Anfield boss said, 'With the freedom he [Gerrard] has now and his quality going forward, he's unstoppable. Stevie now has the same freedom he had as a right-winger when he came inside. He's enjoying it because he knows he can go forward with no problem.

'The understanding with Fernando is also very good. He knows that when he goes forward he can pick him out easily. It could be that they bring out the best in each other. Of course, he still needs to help out the midfielders but it's not the same as running back 30 or 40 metres. He knows what we expect from him and he is playing well in virtually every game. Every manager talks to their players about what to do but he is clever enough to know that.'

So pleased was Benitez with his side's recent performances that it also appeared he had decided to shelve his controversial rotation policy, at least for the time being. 'For me, the key is that, because we only have two competitions to go for, I won't change too many players, so they have to work really hard to get into the team because of that,' he explained. 'When the team's working so hard, it makes it difficult to create chances against us. From now until the end of the season we want to be competing, playing good football, controlling games and winning.'

That was certainly the plan against Inter and, unsurprisingly, Gerrard was backing Torres to make the difference at the San Siro, hailing his partner in goals as the world's best. 'He's brilliant, fantastic. I wouldn't swap him for any other striker anywhere in the world,' said Gerrard. 'He has been massive for us and gives us so many different options up front. He's banging them in and always looks a threat every time he plays.

'The lad who comes into their side for [the suspended] Marco Materazzi will not be looking forward to his 90 minutes against Fernando. We will be looking to hit them on the counter-attack and Torres plays that game better than anyone around. Not only can you stick the ball over the top and let him chase it, but he can make things happen himself like he did against Marseille earlier in the tournament, when we needed to win in France to go through to the last 16.

'He roasted Materazzi in the first leg. He [Materazzi] might think he was hard done by to be sent off but he could have been booked for a bad tackle before he had one yellow, never mind the second one. It shows how easily Torres' pace and strength unsettled a World Cup winner.

'You can play him on his own or with a partner and he just adapts perfectly. He's certainly made life tough for the foreign boys coming to England now. When you look at the impact he has made in just seven months here, it means that no one now can make excuses about needing time to settle.

'I feel England suits him even better than Spain. He suits the constant flow and the rough and tumble of the Premier League better than the stop-start technical La Liga. He is just a kid really in football terms, and he is going to get better and better. That is a frightening thought, but not for us. It's frightening for the defences he is going to be coming up against.'

That bullish confidence of Gerrard's could not help but rub off on his team-mates around him. Gerrard, of course, had inspired that incredible revival against AC Milan three years previously as Liverpool came from 3–0 down in the Champions League final to take the trophy after a penalty shoot-out. That night in Istanbul cemented his love affair with the competition and he had no intention of allowing this year's adventure to end in Italy, although he accepted that, even though Liverpool had been in scintillating form in recent weeks, they would have to raise their game still further if they were to progress to the quarter-finals. He added, 'We will have to play as well as we have done anywhere this season now. We are facing another big test. We did the job in the first leg and did it brilliantly but we have qualified for nothing yet.

'The last eight is 90 minutes away and we might have to play better than we did in the first match. They are going to fly out at us from the first whistle but we can defend all night if we have to. But we also believe we will worry the hell out of them. They will be reluctant to over-commit against us because they got nothing at Anfield. They got no change from our defence, no possession and no time to settle. We will be going for them again because we know we can score there and kill off the tie. I will relish playing in the San Siro, I've never done it before and it's another one off my list.

'Fans like going to famous grounds to watch us, and as a player I want to play in the cathedrals around Europe. I've played in the Nou Camp and a lot of famous stadiums around the world, but this is a new one for a few of us. If we get the attitude right, take our chances and believe in ourselves it will be another night to remember.'

And a night to remember it most certainly was, as Liverpool booked their place in the quarter-finals thanks to yet another terrific goal from Torres. The centre-forward collected Fabio Aurelio's low ball into the penalty area, turned defender Christian Chivu expertly and unleashed a fearsome right-foot shot into the bottom left-hand corner of the net.

It was a goal worthy of winning any match and secured the club's last-eight berth to leave Benitez beaming. He said, 'We knew the first game would be important. Today the idea was to compete, counter-attack and we knew we couldn't make mistakes. So I am really pleased with the performance of the side in both games.

'In the first year I was here, no one thought we could win the final but we did. For me, the important thing is for the team to be in the Champions League every year. I do not mind who we face in the next round. I will wait for the draw and enjoy this victory now.'

And Benitez reserved special mention for his team's goalscoring hero, adding, 'We have a lot of confidence in him [Torres]. He is a threat for defenders, that is clear. We are really pleased with how he has adapted to the Premier League and we are waiting for more goals. Twenty-six is good but he can get more. He is a player with a good mentality and wants to improve every game.'

The *Daily Telegraph*'s chief football correspondent Henry Winter, meanwhile, was even more fulsome in his praise of El Niño. He wrote, 'Red Square could live up to its name this year. Liverpool continued their route march towards the Moscow climax of the

Champions League, reaching the quarter-finals with a performance spiced by another example of Fernando Torres' brilliance. Torres' goals are works of science as well as art, and this was so brutal, so devastating to lingering Italian ambition that one half expected a white towel to come fluttering out of the home dug-out.'

And Winter's view of Torres was echoed by Liverpool stars past and present. Current colleague Dirk Kuyt said, 'Fernando is just special. It is amazing to score this many goals in his first season in England. He is getting them in the league and in Europe; he is doing a great job for the team. He will only get better and better. Other teams now are very worried by him, but you could see with the way he put away his one chance of the night [against Inter] just how dangerous he is. The rest of the players seem to think he will score in every game, and the way it is going, that is starting to happen.'

Former Anfield hero Tommy Smith was happy to compare the Spanish ace with Liverpool legends of yesteryear. He told the club's website, 'Torres is up there with the best Anfield strikers of the past 50 years. Roger Hunt was a tremendous player and could score from anywhere – a bit like Torres, who is one of the best I have seen in a red shirt. In the 1970s you had Kevin Keegan, a good link player who was always on hand to accept chances. Ian Rush had a great time scoring for the Reds in partnership with Kenny Dalglish. I always said when he was sold to Juventus that they forgot to take Dalglish, too, because he made so many of Rushie's goals.

'Torres has a special ingredient we have not seen for some time. He has the ability to glide past defenders with effortless pace and often places the ball home rather than using power. What a talent.'

Torres continued his goalscoring streak in the next match against Reading, scoring for a fourth game in a row, as the Reds made it seven wins on the bounce with a 2–1 victory over the Royals at Anfield. It was a far cry from the disappointing afternoon in December when Benitez had appeared to raise the white flag of surrender as far as his side's title hopes were concerned. They still trailed leaders Manchester United and Arsenal by a full eight points, but they were at least holding firm in fourth, with only local rivals Everton in genuine contention to deny them that Champions League place.

And Torres' latest goal saw him achieve yet another landmark in his first season at the club, becoming the first player since Robbie Fowler to score 20 league goals in a single campaign. The *Daily Mirror* reported, 'Fernando Torres became the first Anfield player to score 20 league goals for the club since the great Robbie Fowler achieved the feat 12 years ago. His goalscoring needs to be put into context. This is his first season in the maelstrom of the Premier League, and yet he has already achieved what strikers such as Michael Owen and previous record signings Stan Collymore, Emile Heskey and Djibril Cissé failed to do at Anfield. He has 27 now in all competitions for Liverpool and will surely join the greats of Fowler, Ian Rush, John Aldridge and Roger Hunt in modern times of reaching 30 goals for the club. That is some list, and Torres can be proud to be mentioned in the same breath as those true greats.'

Team-mate Jamie Carragher was also thrilled with the Spaniard's success. He told the Liverpool website, 'To get 20 league goals says it all really and just goes to show what he is all about. It's a long time since Robbie did it and it's something we've needed for a while now. It takes a special player to achieve it and that's just what Fernando is. He is capable of scoring a lot of goals for us and you'd back him to go on and get many more in a Liverpool shirt. It's some achievement when you think it's his first year in England and, like I say, hopefully there will be even more to come from him this season.

'It was a great header he scored, too [against Reading]. I was just behind him and it wasn't easy to get up and direct it goalwards like that. People probably don't think of Torres scoring headers but he is good in the air and capable of scoring all types of goals. He's in great form at the moment and long may it continue.'

That win was the Reds' fifth in a row in the Premier League, and their seventh consecutive victory in all competitions, but any lingering hopes that they may yet mount a late challenge for the title were dashed in their very next fixture. And it will have come as a crushing blow to Liverpool fans that those faint hopes were finally extinguished at Manchester United of all places. But even though they went into the game in the middle of a terrific run, scoring plenty of goals and conceding very few, they once more came unstuck against Sir Alex Ferguson's men.

Goals from Wes Brown, Cristiano Ronaldo and Nani secured a 3–0 win for the reigning champions and finally laid to rest the slim chance Liverpool had of overhauling the leaders at the top of the Premier League. The game, though, was overshadowed by a red card for Javier Mascherano, who picked up two yellow cards, the second of which was shown to him by referee Steve Bennett because the Argentine midfielder appeared to be arguing with him. Mascherano, however, insisted he had done nothing wrong and was merely questioning the official as to why a foul had not been awarded for an aggressive challenge on Ryan Babel.

He said, 'I do not know why I was sent off. I asked the referee what was happening. I did not swear, I was not aggressive and I did not confront him. All I did was ask him what was happening, nothing else. So when he showed me the second yellow card and sent me off I could not believe it. I am sorry for my team-mates because that meant we went down to ten men and that made things even more difficult for us.'

Whatever the rights or wrongs of that dismissal, it left his side with a mountain to climb but it was one they were unable to scale. And their task was certainly not helped with Torres forced to limp out of the action with injuries to an ankle and to his ribs.

With the Premier League title now completely out of reach, as it probably was even before the defeat to United, it left the Reds with just fourth place to aim for. But if ever they needed an incentive to dust themselves down, pick themselves up and get on with the job of securing that fourth spot it came in their very next game against their nearest challengers and local rivals, Everton.

Torres' injury forced him to miss Spain's first training session as they prepared for a friendly clash with Italy, but Liverpool boss Benitez was confident his striker would be fit enough to play for his country, and then take his place for his club in the Merseyside derby.

Certainly, it was a game he would not want to miss, having been forced to sit out the season's first meeting at Goodison Park after straining abductor muscles, an injury he first sustained while away on international duty. Benitez said, 'We saw that every time he went for the ball on Sunday [against Manchester United] he was put under a lot of pressure, but at this moment I think he will be fit for Sunday [against Everton]. He lost one day with Spain but he's back now and I think he will be ready for their game, and hopefully he'll then be available for us at the weekend.'

In the end, Benitez need not have worried as his star striker reported back fit and ready for action after international duty. And the Anfield boss knew that was an important boost as his side looked to open up a gap between themselves and Everton for that fourth position. He said, 'Torres is a player with a lot of quality and confidence and it's always important to have your top scorer playing. He is always a threat to any defence. He is playing well and scoring goals and if the team can help him then I think he will score at least 30 goals this season.'

And former Anfield star Jimmy Case also felt Torres could be the difference between the Merseyside teams. He told the club's website, 'The derby is always very special and this is a big game with fourth place up for grabs. The key man for me will be Torres. He always gives Liverpool the edge every time he plays. He is a superb player and he gives them an extra dimension with his pace and forward running. And once he sets off in his stride running at the opposition he is so difficult to catch.'

And Case's prediction was to be proved right as Torres provided the decisive finish in only the seventh minute of the match to earn Liverpool their eighth victory in nine games and move them five points clear of Everton in the race for fourth place. It was the

Spaniard's 28th goal of the season, and Liverpool's 100th. It was fitting that he should be the man to register that landmark and his winner left Benitez delighted. He said, 'To score 28 goals, 21 in the league, in your first season is not easy for anyone, especially for a player coming to a different country. I think the understanding between Gerrard and Torres is good so we tried to use these two key players.'

Fernando himself was also thrilled with his derby-day winner. He said, 'Last week against Manchester United things did not go well for us but even when we were 3–0 down the fans were still with us and I could hear them singing my name. As a player that makes you feel really good, to know that you have their support, and for that reason my goal in the derby is for them. They were with me when things were going badly so it is good to be able to score a goal that will make them happy. To score the winner in my first derby is fantastic. It is very important to me that the fans are happy because, if they are happy, I am happy.'

It was clear that the Liverpool fans loved Torres, and there was no doubt the feeling was mutual. He continued, 'I always feel confident that I can score at Anfield. I've got 19 Premier League goals here now which is fantastic for me, and I seem to score most of those in front of the Kop. I don't know why that is, but I'm always scoring at that end. It must be something about the stand, it is just different. I think 15 of those 19 goals have come in front of the Kop, and I always feel confident when I'm facing that end of the pitch.'

His goal against Everton meant he had now scored in six consecutive home games, equalling a club record he now shared with Fred Pagnam (1919), Roger Hunt (1964), Ian Rush (1983) and Michael Owen (1999).

But there was no doubt that the winner against Liverpool's Goodison Park rivals was among the highlights of his collection. 'To score the winner in my first derby is fantastic', the then 24-year-old told the Liverpool website. 'But the victory was the most important thing and Everton are further away than before, and we are on target for the top four and can concentrate on the Champions League now.'

It was the perfect end to his first Merseyside derby and he added, 'It was amazing. The fans are very happy now. There was very good support for both teams. A derby game is always different from the others. It's an important game for the fans, and you can feel all through the week building up to the game that it's a special game. Beating Everton always makes the fans happy.'

Beating Everton had clearly made everyone connected with the club happy and it was the perfect preparation for another massive challenge – a Champions League quarter-final date with Arsenal. And with all four English teams through to the last eight, the rest of Europe, it appeared, was running scared. Even as Barcelona star Lionel Messi got ready for his side's meeting with German outfit Schalke, he admitted it was the English contingent of whom he was most apprehensive, with Torres being singled out for particular praise. The little Argentine wizard said, 'Manchester United are very good and Cristiano Ronaldo is a great player who I watch a lot. The other top English teams – Arsenal, Chelsea and Liverpool – are capable of success, too, because they have special players like Cesc

Fabregas, Didier Drogba and Fernando Torres. The best Premier League clubs also have the experience of doing well in the Champions League.'

Messi knew, though, that he would not have to face Liverpool until at least the final. The Reds' prize for getting past Arsenal, which in itself promised to be a severe examination, would be a semi-final meeting with Chelsea, the third time in just four years the Premier League rivals had met in the knockout stages of the competition.

Before they could worry about that challenge, however, they had to overcome Arsenal. In an extraordinary twist of fate, the two teams would meet each other three times in a week, twice in Europe and once in the Premier League, and it was a series of matches Torres was relishing. He told the assembled media pack ahead of the first Champions League meeting at the Emirates Stadium, 'It's an important game for us and an important game for the fans. There are three games to play against Arsenal but for now we are just concentrating on the first one. The most important thing for us is to win this first game and then we can look ahead to the other 180 minutes. We have respect for Arsenal and I'm sure they have respect for us. I'm not sure they'll fear us but they will respect us. We are always strong in Europe and hopefully we can be again in this game.'

Torres would surely be a central figure in the contests and his link up with England international Gerrard, which had so far yielded 47 goals between them, promised to be perhaps the key ingredient as to who came out on top at the end of what was sure to be a pulsating week of football.

The Spaniard said of his Liverpool colleague, 'He's easy to play with because he's one of the best midfielders in the world, if not the best. You always want to play with the best players in the big competitions. I have improved already as a player at Liverpool because of my team-mates and because of my manager. Since my first day here, I've felt at home. It's my best season so far in terms of scoring goals but I'm not going to set myself a target for the rest of the season. I just want to help my team-mates win trophies.'

Arsenal manager Arsène Wenger certainly knew his side had to be wary of the dangers posed by Torres if their own European season was not to be derailed. He said, 'I rate Torres. I believe he had quite a good start after a spell when he was in and out. Since he has been back on a regular basis, he is extremely dangerous. He is quick, strong, brave and that's the kind of competition you want to keep quiet in the Champions League. You must be particularly careful when he is away from home. You do not want to give him any counter-attacking chances. He and Steven Gerrard are both very quick on the break.'

Wenger, though, denied that he had tried to sign the Spaniard before he moved to Anfield. 'We have known about him for a long time, but I never tried to sign him,' he insisted. 'We were interested when he first started at Atletico Madrid, but we never made any offer.'

The clash at the Emirates promised to be a rip-roaring beginning to the trilogy of games and Wenger added, 'When you play a "local" team in the European Cup it is a test of character. We know we can do it, but who wants it the most? Against an English team the competition is always different. You come back more to a formula –

the mental strengths of the two teams will make all the difference in the game. We know each other well, so there are two things which will make the difference – the quantity of the mental strengths available in the teams and how well the players who can make a decision perform.

'We play each other three times in six days and it will be a case of who is ready again. You know in this game – a direct knockout – the goal conceded at home is the killer. In a league game, you think even if you concede a goal you can still win it. So you have to be organised, cautious and make sure you defend well first before you attack. Against Liverpool, we will have to win the physical battle as well. They can raise their game and it is a team which at home can dig deep and produce a result.'

And Liverpool proved in north London that, as well as being able to dig deep and produce a result at home, they could do the same away. They recovered quickly from the setback of conceding a goal to Emmanuel Adebayor after 23 minutes by bouncing straight back to equalise through Dirk Kuyt just three minutes later. And that was how the game stayed, meaning Liverpool had got that priceless away goal and they were now very much the favourites to go through to the last four.

Not that Benitez agreed with that assessment, saying, 'I don't think we are favourites. When you play against Arsenal, you know they can score in any stadium, but we are in a good position as we are playing at Anfield with our supporters which makes a massive difference.

'They had plenty of possession and we had to play on the counter-attack and work really hard in defence. Arsenal are a good team, they were attacking and we had to defend as we can – sometimes deep – and try to play on the break. We had two or three chances but we gave away the ball at the last pass and that could have been the difference.

'It was really important for us [to equalise quickly] because, if you play against Arsenal, concede a goal and cannot score soon, it becomes difficult. The away goal is always important because we know if we can score at home it will be more difficult for them. It's a good situation for us – still difficult but better than before.'

The second meeting between the two, again at the Emirates, offered few clues as to the final outcome of their European clash as both managers chose to make wholesale changes, with Torres among several key players rested by Benitez, before eventually being given a ten-minute run-out at the end. And once more honours ended even in a 1–1 draw.

What was most interesting, perhaps, was the performance of Peter Crouch, who was chosen to replace Torres as the focal point of the Liverpool attack. He is a player Arsenal had struggled with in the past, and they did so again, and his goal was a fitting reward for his all-round display. And if the England striker was trying to send a message to Benitez that he merited more playing time it was one that clearly got through, because, when the Anfield boss named his side for the third meeting with the Gunners, and the crucial Champions League decider, Crouch was included in the starting line-up alongside Torres and Kuyt in a selection clearly designed to go for goals.

Even though they knew a goalless draw would be enough to send them through to the semi-finals, Benitez was determined his side would go through in style. He said, 'I think it will be a different game compared to the last two for two reasons – one is that we are playing at Anfield and that is a massive difference, and the other thing is that they need to win, so it could be an attacking game. We need to win also, we don't want a 0–0 draw. We prefer to score and we prefer to win. We know that Arsenal can score away from home.'

Liverpool at Anfield on a big European night are a tough proposition for any opponent, as many have found to their cost down the years. And on the eve of the game, Fernando explained how he and his team-mates got an extra special lift from the Anfield crowd on nights like that. The young Spaniard had first experienced that amazing European atmosphere in the home leg of the last-16 clash against Inter Milan in February and he was hoping to feel that kind of inspiration again against the Gunners. He said, 'The game against Inter was fantastic. They are a very good team so to beat them gave us a lot of confidence. The atmosphere was incredible. The fans sang for the whole game and their support was one of the main reasons why we were able to get the victory.

'Every ground we play at you can hear the Liverpool fans singing their songs and supporting the team and it makes you feel really good. But European nights are the most special of all. I was told about them when I first joined Liverpool but now I have enjoyed them for myself I just want more and more of them.

'When I hear the fans sing the song they have for me it gives me a great feeling. It seems like it is getting louder all the time and, as a player, it is really good to know you are supported this way. Hopefully we will repay their support by getting the result the fans want.

'We were pleased with the result last week because we got an away goal and we came away with a draw. But that does not mean this game will be straightforward. Arsenal are a very good team and we will have to play well if we are to beat them. We have confidence because we are playing well but that does not mean we are taking anything for granted. People are saying we are favourites but for me the tie is quite balanced. We have played Arsenal three times this season and each time the score has been 1–1 so that shows that there is not that much between the two teams.

'Earlier this season, Arsenal came to Anfield and got a draw and we have just drawn two games at the Emirates. The two teams know each other well and we respect each other so this game could be just as tight as the previous games.'

For all the talk of tight, cagey affairs, though, the match was anything but. In fact, it turned out to be something of a classic as Liverpool ran out 4–2 winners in a pulsating game with goals from Hyypia, Torres, Gerrard and Babel. But that final scoreline tells only half the tale as Liverpool recovered from going a goal down on the night to lead 2–1, and 3–2 on aggregate, with just six minutes remaining. But then Emmanuel Adebayor pounced to make it 2–2 on the night and give the visitors the advantage on the away goals rule. Incredibly, though, Liverpool struck back with two goals in the final four minutes to book their place in the last four.

'It was a great night and a fantastic game, with six goals. Everyone is happy,' said Benitez. 'Of course, the amazing support here at Anfield is a big factor. We started very badly in the first half but the second half was much better. The players always respond to the crowd, and tonight was no exception. I was anxious of course when Arsenal made it 2–2, and particularly disappointed with the way Arsenal scored, but I am very happy with the reaction of the players.'

It was an extraordinary night at Anfield and an occasion that Fernando admitted he would never forget. He said, 'It was the biggest night of my career and I came to Liverpool for nights like this. It is unbelievable – the high tempo of both teams, the fans, everything.

'It was special for all of us because of the work that we put in. To score four goals against a very good side is a good achievement for us and we are all very proud. It was a great game for Liverpool and for Arsenal but the most important thing for us is that we are now in the semi-finals.'

Fernando's goal took his tally for the season to 29, but he confessed that it was his most memorable so far. He added, 'I don't know what makes this goal so special, but scoring there, in front of the Kop, is fantastic. The stand is so high, so impressive. I think I have scored half of my goals there. I hope I will continue to score important goals there.

'It's impressive how much people respect you. They want to see you playing in each game so that makes you need to prove yourself on the pitch. For me, it fills me with pride that in a quick period of time they created a song for me and they sing it to me during almost every game. It's important for a footballer that the fans consider you one of theirs.'

But the Spanish superstar admitted he feared his side's European adventure was over after Adebayor's goal made it 2–2 on the night. 'Yes, I thought it was finished,' he admitted. 'There were only a few minutes left but, with the magic of Anfield, the players were able to score two more goals. Liverpool is special. It is a special team, with special fans and a special city and today I am very happy to live in this city and to play for this club.'

That win set up the remarkable prospect of a third semi-final meeting with Chelsea in just four years, and Fernando knew it would be another titanic struggle against one of Liverpool's Premier League rivals. He continued, 'We know that Chelsea are also a very good team but we will see if we can make it to the final. The English teams are the strongest at the moment so we know it will be difficult. We now have two games against Chelsea and our target is to finish in the top four in the Premier League and to win the Champions League.'

Before that encounter with the men from Stamford Bridge, however, Liverpool had league games against Blackburn and Fulham to focus on as they looked to consolidate fourth place in the table. A 3–1 win over Blackburn was a great start, a game in which Torres reached the milestone of 30 goals, a phenomenal achievement in his first season in English football. It also made him the first player in the club's illustrious history to score in seven consecutive home games and, as he reflected on his debut campaign, even he was struggling to believe things had gone quite so well. 'You have to enjoy it when everything is fine,' he said in an interview on the club's website. 'I want people to always remember me here. It is what I was dreaming of. I expected it to take more time. Achieving all that in the first season is amazing.

'The team have been working very well and helped me a lot. Settling has been very easy and you can see it on the pitch. I have been helped with everything. Every player feels important thanks to the fans, from Pepe [Reina] to the strikers, because they sing their names and support them.

'People respect you a lot here. For example, I was in a supermarket this morning and the fans were very calm, did not jump on me, they just congratulated me and asked me if they could take pictures with me. There are plenty of Everton fans in the streets but there are no problems. We have fans around the world and we can see it every time we play away. It is a different culture than in Spain, obviously, and the rivalry with Manchester United and Liverpool is impressive.'

With 30 goals in total, 22 of them in the Premier League, Fernando was within touching distance of Ruud van Nistelrooy's record of 23 in a debut season having moved to England from overseas. And it was a record he wanted.

'I am proud and want to beat every record I can,' he added. 'I feel important in the team. The game against Chelsea gave me confidence to carry on. I have never scored 30 goals in a season in my career and I have made it here. I have been helped by the team's style of football.'

His team-mates were in no doubt that he would set a new benchmark and that, when he did, it would be a record he truly merited. 'Yes, I think he deserves that,' said Dirk Kuyt. 'He has scored many goals already and is playing really well for us. We still have a few games to go and, with Fernando on fire as he has been, I see no reason why he won't reach that target and beat the record. We will have to wait and see but he definitely has the quality to score more than 23 league goals this season. Like I say, it seems like he can score in every game.

'To take the record from someone like Van Nistelrooy would be a great achievement. He was absolutely fabulous for Manchester United in that first season and most of the years to follow. Van Nistelrooy is a great striker but Fernando is only going to get better and better. I can only see him scoring more goals.

'He is always a threat for opposing defenders. It is unbelievable just how well he has adapted to the Premier League and settled in so easily at Liverpool. Speaking from my own experience, I know how difficult it is to come to a big club from a new country. For Dutch people, who often speak English already, it is probably much easier than for a Spanish player who may not know the language right away, as was the case with Fernando. We've seen over the years that many players who don't know the language need a little more time to adapt. For example, someone like Lucas Leiva has needed a few more months than Fernando to get used to things here but that is a testament to just how quickly Fernando has taken to everything.

'He is scoring in almost every game now, which is a pleasure for everyone else in the team. It means we are confident of scoring every time we play. If we get it right defensively, this means we have a good chance of winning every game.'

And Kuyt revealed that the rest of the players at Anfield were happy to play second fiddle to Torres and Gerrard, just so long as that meant the team kept winning. 'People often speak about Fernando and Stevie simply because they are the best players in the team,' added Kuyt on liverpoolfc.tv. 'But the rest of the team has to work really hard to enable their ability to score goals and do all the things they do. In that sense, every member of the team is important to allow Stevie and Fernando to keep producing the levels they do. Whether they score the goals or not, we are happy as everybody is aiming for the same objective, to win as many trophies as possible.

'If we keep working hard as a team we know we can still win games even if we don't play our best football. And with players like Stevie and Fernando in your team, they can always decide a game for us.'

Torres was given a breather for the next game, a trip to Fulham which Liverpool won 2–0, to ensure he was in the best possible shape for the visit of Chelsea just three days later. It was a fixture that gripped the nation and revived memories of the controversial previous clashes between the pair, notably the 2005 semi-final win at Anfield when Luis Garcia was credited with the winning goal despite the visitors' protests that the ball had not crossed the line. So it would be fair to say there was a lot more than merely domestic bragging rights at stake as the two sides prepared to lock horns.

The other semi-final saw Manchester United meet Barcelona and Torres admitted it would be wonderful to take on the Catalan giants, a team against whom he had enjoyed plenty of success with Atletico Madrid, in the final. 'Manchester United's level is very high [at the moment],' he said. 'They have not lost many points in the league.

They have won all the big games they had to do in Europe without any problem so they are definitely the team to beat.

'People in Barcelona will see what they are made of. The game should be spectacular because they are both attacking sides. We want to play in the final and facing Barça would be ideal. But first of all we have to beat Chelsea and that is not going to be easy.'

And having played in both La Liga and the Premier League, how did Fernando feel the leagues matched up? 'The top four teams are great in England and in Spain, but I think that the mid-table ones are more competitive in La Liga,' he said. 'In Spain, we are more technical and slower. Here they are very dynamic and never stop. As far as the Premier League is concerned, there is a world [of difference] between the top four and the other teams.'

Both previous semi-finals between the pair had been incredibly tight affairs, with Liverpool winning by that solitary Garcia goal over two legs in 2005, and then winning on penalties in 2007 after both games had ended in 1-1 draws. On both those occasions, Liverpool had played the second leg at home, with the Anfield crowd roaring them on to victory, and on the eve of the first leg against Chelsea, Torres called on them once more to be the team's 12th man. 'The atmosphere against Arsenal [in the quarter-final] was fantastic and it is hard to believe that it is possible for it to be better than that,' he said. 'At the end of the game, I looked around the ground and all I could see was red and white flags and scarves and the noise was incredible. I have said it brought tears to my eyes and that is true. It is hard to believe that there are any more special places in football than Anfield on a European night.'

While the majority of his team-mates had had the experience of facing Chelsea in a big European semi-final, this would be the first time on that stage for Torres. And he admitted he could not wait. 'I have spoken to all of the players who were here on those nights and they have all told me that the atmosphere was the best they have ever played in,' he continued. 'It is incredible to think that it could be any better than it was against Arsenal and I cannot wait.

'People talk about the power of Anfield and it is true, it really does exist. Some clubs have legends that are not true but, at Liverpool, the legend of the crowd is true. I know because I have experienced it. Against Inter Milan the noise was fantastic but it was even better when we played Arsenal.

'I am really excited about this match because I know the fans will deliver. Then it is up to the players on the pitch to do the same. We know Chelsea are a very good side. They are still in the race for the league title and are in the semi-finals of the European Cup so you have to give them the respect they deserve. We also know that they will be very difficult opponents for us because they have proved that many times in the past and I'm sure they will want to beat us after what happened in the previous two semi-finals.

'They are very hard to beat. If you look at the players in their team, the likes of Cech, Terry, Carvalho, Essien and Drogba make them very strong. But we also have good players and we have shown in the past and also this season that we are able to compete with them.

'It will be physical and a strong match. We both know we are very close to the final and that means all the players on both teams will be motivated. I do not think there is a great deal between the two teams because we have played each other twice in the league this season and both games ended in a draw. But we managed to win against Arsenal in the last round and we have taken a lot of confidence from that because it proved we can beat a top English side in this competition. There is a winning mentality at Liverpool. I look around in the dressing room before a game, and in the face of every player and every coach you see the winning expectation. Now we have two games to get to the final. We know we can do it.'

Liverpool defender Jamie Carragher, like Torres, was expecting another tense tussle, but reckoned the Reds might have the ace in the pack in the shape of the Spanish scoring sensation. He told the media, 'Last season, I said the team needed a player who could add that "X" factor. We wanted someone who could do something unbelievable and hurt the opposition when they were not expecting it. All the top teams have a player like that. We've relied on Stevie Gerrard to do that for us for a long time – but now Fernando has added another dimension to the side. For me, he has to be the best striker in the world. His goal against Arsenal in the quarter-final second leg came out of nothing. It was a sharp turn and smashing shot. I'm delighted we've got him.'

The win over Fulham the previous weekend had all but secured fourth spot so Liverpool could concentrate all their energies on Chelsea, but Carragher knew the Londoners would be out for revenge. He continued, 'We have beaten them three times in semi-finals when you include the FA Cup in 2006, so they will be desperate to turn us over. Hopefully, we can keep that run going. But we realise they are doing well at the moment and it will be difficult to stop them. I think it will be as close as the last two European clashes. It's always been that way against them and I wouldn't expect it to be any different.'

Former Liverpool star Michael Thomas also reckoned Torres could be the difference between the two sides. He told the Liverpool website, 'I'd love to see us go all the way, but it will be tough. Many people are looking at it thinking it'll be third time lucky for Chelsea and you do start to wonder whether we can beat them in yet another semi-final. But we can do it and the team is even better than it was in the last two meetings in 2005 and 2007. This time we've got Fernando Torres in our team and, for me, he can make the difference. He proved again against Arsenal [in the quarter-final] that he's top class. He was quiet all night long and then suddenly produced a moment of brilliance to turn the game back in Liverpool's favour. That's what great players can do.'

The Chelsea camp also admitted they were extremely conscious of the dangers Torres posed to their hopes of finally ending their Champions League hoodoo and reaching the final for the first time in the club's history. Manager Avram Grant said, 'We see him score almost every Saturday so we don't need a special video on him. He is a good player and Liverpool are a good team, especially when they play in Europe. But we are also a good team.'

And Blues captain John Terry also spoke of the need to nullify Torres in the same press briefing. He said, 'They've always had the backbone of Stevie and Carra, and that's been tremendously important for them. But now they've added Torres and he gets goals.

'Torres is a very good player. His movement is fantastic and the

162

Right: Torres swaps his kit for a suit at a press conference at the Vicente Calderon Stadium.

Below: Torres faces a barrage of microphones as he confirms his record-breaking move to Liverpool.   © *PA Photos*

Smiles all round as Torres poses for the first time in Liverpool's famous red shirt. © *Clevamedi*

Jumping for joy as he scores the first of his two goals in a crucial Champions League win over Porto at Anfield.

© Clevamedia

Above: The ecstasy of scoring against Arsenal in Liverpool's Champions League quarter-final victory.

Below: The agony of losing in the semi-finals to Chelsea. Although Torres got the better of Michael Essien to score Liverpool's first goal at Stamford Bridge under Rafa Benitez, he was later forced off injured and could only watch as the Reds lost 4–3 on aggregate. © *Clevamedia*

way from the pressures of the Premier League, Torres likes nothing better than
laxing with girlfriend Olalla.

© *Rex Features*

Torres is a study in concentration as Spain beat Sweden at Euro 2008.

© Rex Features

bove: Spain and Germany get to grips with each other in the Euro 2008 Final.

elow: Torres writes his name into Spain's history books as he scores the winning goal gainst Germany to earn his country their first major honour for 44 years.

© Rex Features/© Clevamedia

Spain reign as Torres and his team-mates lift the Euro 2008 trophy.

© Clevamed

likes of Stevie and the other midfielders can find him at any time. We'll have to be very good defensively and if we can keep Torres and Stevie quiet we should be OK. Benitez has bought very well in the last few years. They are a great team who work together. That's what we need to show on the night.'

And Terry admitted that the pain of the two previous last four defeats would drive him and his team-mates on in the search for glory. 'That burning is still there from when we lost to Liverpool on those two occasions, and that will never go away,' he added. 'But we can ease it if we win this semi-final and go on to lift the trophy. But it's not about putting the record straight; it's about what this club can go on to do. It's a massive chance for the players and manager to make history. Forget what's happened [in the past], it's about now.'

Unsurprisingly, the match at Anfield proved to be another close encounter. But Liverpool dominated for long periods and looked to be well worth the 1–0 win they were within touching distance of until disaster struck in the fifth minute of injury time. Full-back John Arne Riise stooped to head clear a low cross but succeeding only in diverting it past goalkeeper Pepe Reina and into the top corner to earn Chelsea a 1–1 draw.

It was a cruel body blow to the Reds and completely shifted the emphasis of the tie. With a home leg to come and an away goal in the bank, Chelsea were now very much the favourites to progress.

Manager Benitez was crestfallen as he faced the media afterwards. He said, 'It is difficult to understand what happened – there were 94 or 95 minutes on the clock. I was really surprised and, of course, very disappointed with the own-goal – those kinds of bouncing balls are very difficult to deal with. The reaction in the dressing room afterwards was one of great disappointment. The only thing we can do now is be positive and think about the next game. We now need to go there and win. It's not easy to create chances in these games but we had three clear chances to score and I am disappointed we did not take them. We have to change our mindset now and be positive for the return at Stamford Bridge.

'My confidence is based on watching the team today. We were on top for a lot of the game, especially at the start of the second half. With a bit of luck we can do it.'

With the return leg just a week away, Benitez again made wholesale changes to the side that travelled to Birmingham in the Premier League and secured a 2–2 draw. But, essentially, that match was almost a distraction before they got back down to the serious business of that Champions League semi-final.

If Liverpool were to triumph in the second leg and book their place in the final in Moscow, they would have to do something they had never managed under Benitez – score at Stamford Bridge. But Liverpool's players were supremely confident they would do that, and were backing Torres to be the man to break their duck.

'We've never played there with Fernando Torres, have we?' replied skipper Gerrard when asked about his side's goalless run in west London. And he remained confident about the Reds' chances of bouncing back from the disappointment of conceding that last-gasp equaliser at Anfield. 'Obviously we're disappointed with the late goal but it's done,' he told the club's website. 'We've got to pick ourselves up. We've got to give it everything we can at Stamford Bridge. We know this tie is not over.

'It's my job as captain to pick the boys up and make sure we're ready. Let people say Chelsea are favourites... let them. We've got to block that out and do what we've got to do. We are confident we can beat Chelsea on their patch. We created the better chances against them in the first leg. I don't think Pepe [Reina] had anything to do besides pick the ball out late on, whereas Petr Cech had to pull off two or three great saves. To be honest, we'd have been disappointed if that game had ended 1–0 when it could have been 2–0.'

Jamie Carragher, as you would expect, was singing from the same hymn sheet as his captain. He said, 'I'm sure the manager will set us up like he always does in Europe and will look to make us hard to beat. We know we need to get a goal but there's no point in doing well at one end of the pitch if we don't do well at the other. We won't be going gung-ho and we won't do anything daft or naive. The thing is, if Chelsea do get a goal, it won't make that much difference because we will still need to score.

'A lot of people are talking about the fact that we haven't scored at Stamford Bridge for a few years but, as Stevie [Gerrard] said, we've never been there with Fernando Torres. He has been the stand-out striker in world football this season and he is capable of scoring against anyone at any time.'

And for his part, Fernando was eagerly anticipating the chance to test himself again against one of Europe's best central defensive partnerships. He said, 'I have wanted to play against guys like John

Terry and Ricardo Carvalho for a long time, and they do me an honour by giving me a tough time. Now I'm going to try to respond to them by getting a couple of goals against Chelsea.

'Everybody dreams about playing in the Champions League, and in the space of a few months I have gone from watching it on TV to having a part in it and I already have plenty of memories. My goal at the San Siro when we beat Inter Milan 1–0, the 4–0 win over Marseille, and my goal in the 4–2 win over Arsenal – now it is the turn of Chelsea.'

And Torres reckoned that Benitez, rightly hailed in many quarters as a tactical master when it came to European football, would prove that point again. By leaving nothing to chance and studying everything in great detail, the striker fully recognised the part his manager had played in ensuring he had a successful first season in England. 'Rafa calculates everything, including runs and flights of the ball, and studies it on his computer,' said Fernando. 'If he tells you to stand five feet from the penalty spot, it's not in your best interests to be six feet from it!

'He'll show you that the extra distance makes the difference between a goal and a missed chance and it has worked for me. The proof for me is I had never scored a club hat-trick in my life before joining Liverpool, but I've since got three, against Reading, Middlesbrough and West Ham.

'Rafa explained everything to me before I even signed – how we would play, and what our aims were. He even gave me a work schedule in advance. He has great powers of seduction, and makes crazy demands on us. At the end of training, when we are all tired, he can still make us repeat routines 20 or 30 times.

'Nobody is sure of his first-team place at Liverpool. Rafa is merciless, and anyone who wants to play in matches has to earn the right in training. It is different to Spain, where only an earthquake can change the pecking order at a club. You soon learn the Liverpool way of doing things. If you train like an amateur you end up dropped to the bench for the next game.'

No one could have accused Liverpool of playing like amateurs at Stamford Bridge but, unfortunately for them, that accusation could not be levelled at Chelsea either. Liverpool did indeed break their scoring duck at Stamford Bridge and, of course, it was Torres who did it, but another absolutely thrilling encounter saw Chelsea win 3-2 on the night after extra-time to complete a 4-3 aggregate win.

It was a night of huge disappointment for the Reds, and for Torres, who was forced out of the action with a hamstring injury just five minutes into extra-time.

Manager Benitez said, 'In extra-time we saw that we were strong enough physically and mentally and had big chances. But the second goal was really difficult and the third goal killed the game. When we scored our first goal, I was really pleased, really confident that we could progress, but now we have to think about the future as we cannot do anything else. I am really proud – we worked really hard until the end.

'I think it would have been a big difference to come here with a 1-0 lead. They are a good team and in the first half they were really good and played with quality. At the end, you cannot change the situation so there are two good teams in the final. We need to keep working and we have two more games which we must try to win and we will improve the squad and try to be closer next season.'

With their European dream over, Liverpool needed to focus their attention now on their remaining two Premier League games in order to secure fourth spot and make certain of their place among the cream of Europe's crop for 2008/09.

Their penultimate fixture, and the last of the season at Anfield, was against Manchester City. Unsurprisingly, following the disappointment of Wednesday night at Stamford Bridge, they were unable to produce their best form. But they did enough to win the game thanks to yet another goal from Torres. It was his 32nd goal of the season, and his 23rd in the Premier League, equalling Ruud van Nistelrooy's record for the most goals by an overseas player in his first season.

Benitez led the tributes afterwards when he said, 'Fernando has been amazing, and he has reached that total without any penalties. Clearly, it will be more difficult for Torres next season; defenders will have watched him and will work on stopping him. But he can improve even from this. He has a strong mentality and he can cope with what defenders do. It will not be easy to score this many goals again, obviously it will be more difficult for him.

'But if he scores a good number of goals and his team-mates, five of whom have scored ten or more this season, also improve and increase their number of goals, it will be OK for us. It is fantastic for the club now and in the future. He will score many more.'

Torres' goal against City meant he had now scored in eight consecutive home games, good enough to equal another record, set by Roger Hunt 46 years previously. Hunt was the last Liverpool player to score in eight games in a row, but he did it in a side playing in the old Second Division.

Whatever the respective merits of the two achievements when placed side by side, it was still a remarkable feat by the Spaniard and he was thrilled to be bracketed in such company as Hunt. He said, 'I'm very proud. I knew about the record before the game and I am pleased to have scored again. Now I will try to do even better next season. The first season is normally always difficult but it has been made easy for me by my team-mates. It's thanks to them that I can keep scoring and keep improving.'

But, while he was delighted with his personal achievements, he felt a large sense of disappointment that the team would be ending the season empty handed. 'We want to win trophies every season,' he added. 'Maybe next season – we will have to keep improving. For the fans, the most important thing is the league because this club has gone too many years without it. Maybe next season. We are a strong team and we can win every game.'

If Liverpool were to finally end their long wait for the league title in 2008/09, Torres was sure to be a key figure, a fact not lost on his Anfield colleagues. Lucas Leiva reflected after the win over City, 'Torres is improving all of the time. He's getting better and better and he's very important to the team. With Torres on the pitch you know you've always got a good chance to score a goal and that's important for the confidence of the team, to know that he is there. He doesn't miss many chances and he's had a great season. Hopefully we will score as many or more goals next season and we can get closer to the title.'

Obviously, all those close to him at Anfield were well aware of his talents, but his performances in recent months also led to England manager Fabio Capello singling him out for praise when he was asked who he would choose as the Premier League's player of the year. The Italian admitted, 'It would be a tough decision between Ronaldo and Torres.'

In the end, it was Cristiano Ronaldo who collected a clean sweep of the individual awards, fittingly enough given his extraordinary feat of scoring 42 goals in a season from a wide position, but Torres did have the consolation of eclipsing Van Nistelrooy's record in the final game of the season. His goal at White Hart Lane in the defeat of Spurs, the second in Liverpool's 2-0 win against the north Londoners, took his final total for the season to 33, with 24 of them in the Premier League. And Benitez revealed after the match that Fernando had pleaded with him to be selected for the trip to Tottenham, even though the Liverpool manager was considering resting him to allow him extra time to prepare for Euro 2008.

Benitez said, 'We were talking about the record before the game. He wanted to play in this game and wanted to score. Always when you sign a player it's difficult to know if they'll settle in the Premier League, but Torres is young and hungry. He wants to be successful for a number of years. He has shown all these things on the pitch. He is a good striker and there are a lot of good strikers in the Premier League. I don't like to say he is the best because other strikers have other skills, but he is the best for us.'

The Spanish boss did admit, however, that even he had been taken by surprise by the success of his young countryman in his debut season in England. 'We analysed the age, condition, quality and mentality of the player before he arrived, so we knew he was a good player. That is why we signed him. But to score more than 30 goals in a first season is a fantastic achievement. It's a surprise for everyone, not because we didn't have confidence in him, but because it's his first year in the Premier League.'

Remarkably, 21 of Torres' 23 league goals had been scored at Anfield, a ground he clearly enjoyed playing at. But Benitez rubbished any suggestion that the striker was incapable of reproducing that sort of form away from home. He said, 'I don't know why so many of his league goals have come at Anfield. For me, it's a surprise because I'd have thought he'd score more goals away because of his pace and he'd get more space and it would be easier for him.

'Maybe it's just a coincidence. But the motivation at Anfield is fantastic because of our supporters. But he's scored at Stamford Bridge and at the San Siro in the Champions League, so he has shown he can score anywhere.'

Whatever the reasons behind his incredible goal ratio at Anfield, one thing was clear – the Liverpool fans absolutely loved him. And the feeling was entirely mutual. 'The supporters back the players, regardless of who is out on the pitch,' said Fernando. 'They enjoy watching their key players play, because Liverpool has great players, but Liverpool will always be a team.

'The fans get behind the side even when things are not working out, and they are always there until the death. That is the major difference with football back in Spain. If a team is not doing well, then it is because the players do not deserve to be wearing the club's colours. At Liverpool, if a player is wearing their shirt, it is because he deserves it. The fans ask for effort and dedication, and their support is something special, something that stays with you.'

It was evident that just as the Liverpool fans had taken Torres to their hearts so he, too, had taken them and the club to his. The man who had always followed the club's fortunes from afar, even while playing for Atletico Madrid, had seemingly found his spiritual home. Although Atletico would always hold a very special place in his affections, the club were never likely to be able to fulfil his ambitions as a player. Liverpool, on the other hand, could.

But, just as there had been regularly during his days in Spain, as the season was coming to a close there was renewed speculation linking him with clubs such as Chelsea and Barcelona, speculation the club were quick to quash. 'Fernando Torres is just not for sale to anyone,' insisted Liverpool's Chief Executive Rick Parry. 'It is as simple as that, really – he is not going anywhere.'

And Fernando was also keen to reassure supporters that he would be staying at Anfield. 'I have no intention of leaving,' he insisted. 'It is an honour to be linked to clubs like Barcelona, Chelsea or Arsenal, but I am not thinking about a change and I want to continue playing for Liverpool for many years to come. I want to say very clearly that I'm not on the market and it is my desire to continue at Liverpool. I am very happy at Liverpool and want to carry on.

'I have been able to enjoy every minute [of my first year] at a club where things have gone well. I have been part of a team where every player shares the same goals and where a player can rely on the support of his team-mates. I have also worked with a manager who believed in me. It was the combination of all these factors. We have to focus our energies to give the little step we need to get to the top teams. If we only improve the team a little, we are going to manage to do so.'

6

SPAIN REIGN
AT LAST

After a superb first season at Anfield, Fernando Torres could have been forgiven for hoping for a rest. But there was to be no lengthy break from the stresses of top-level football. If anything, they were to increase as he immediately turned his attentions away from domestic matters in England to the international stage with Spain as he prepared for Euro 2008.

Following their disappointing performance at the 2006 World Cup finals in Germany, the Spanish were desperate to succeed in Austria and Switzerland and finally rid themselves of the tag of the 'nearly men' of international football.

They had not tasted success as a country since the European Championship of 1964, 44 long years previously and, despite having many fine players and more often than not being among the favourites when tournaments got under way, they had consistently under-achieved, often being criticised for folding under pressure. So it was against this backdrop and with high expectation from their long-suffering supporters at home that Torres and his international team-mates prepared to take on Europe's best.

Spain had reached the finals as winners of qualifying Group F but, in the early stages of the qualification process, it looked as though they would not make it to the finals at all. And it certainly looked as though, if they did, coach Luis Aragones would not be there with them.

After a confident start with a 4–0 win over minnows Liechtenstein, Spain then lost their next two games, away to Northern Ireland and Sweden, and the pressure on Aragones intensified significantly. Typically, however, the gruff coach responded as his many critics would have expected him to. He insisted at the time, 'Why should I have to step down? When you lose two important games things are obviously difficult, but I've spent a long time in football and dealt with situations like this before.'

In the final analysis, Aragones was proved right. Spain dropped just two more points, in a 1–1 draw away in Iceland, and they won eight of their remaining nine matches to finish two points ahead of Sweden at the top of the group as both countries reached the finals.

Torres, by his own high standards, had a relatively quiet qualifying campaign, scoring only two goals in Spain's 12 matches, although he did miss a number of games through injury. But there was no doubt that, if Spain were to be successful at the finals, he would have a vital role to play. And certainly his Liverpool team-mates were expecting him to shine on the big stage. Finnish central defender Sami Hyypia told the Liverpool website, 'Torres is always a handful as his opponents at Euro 2008 will soon discover. It is quite unbelievable that he scored so many goals in his first season [in England] because it's not easy to come to the Premier League and be successful right away. I knew that he was a quality player, but what has surprised me is that he was very physical. I couldn't believe how much he liked to get involved when he first joined.

'He is very strong and doesn't avoid any contact, not even in training with his mates at Liverpool. I tried to prepare him for the strength in the Premier League as much as possible but I think he always had it in him – he's a bit of a hard man.'

Hyypia's long-time central defensive partner Jamie Carragher also reckoned the free-scoring forward could be the key for his country. 'Torres will go there [to Euro 2008] as the best striker in the world and hopefully he will prove that with Spain,' said Carragher. 'If he does, it will bode well for us next season. He could be the difference for Spain. If you want to go close to winning it you have to have someone who can go close to being leading scorer in the tournament and there's no question that Torres is capable. Spain have got other strikers as well, like David Villa, but they will be looking to Fernando to get them five or six goals and if he performs as well as he has done for us then I'm sure he can do that.'

And Spain's potential opponents in Austria and Switzerland were also well aware of the dangers posed by the Anfield ace. Italy captain Fabio Cannavaro, who had previously played against Torres in La Liga, felt the striker had taken his game to a new level in England following his move 12 months previously. The Real Madrid defender said, 'Fernando Torres has made an incredible improvement. Last year, I saw him as a bit of a softie but then he went to the Premier League, where you can't be a softie, and he exploded.'

His Anfield colleagues in the Spanish squad also confessed that they were looking for Torres to inspire the country to great heights in the finals, with defender Alvaro Arbeloa stressing that El Niño approached the start of the tournament as the best striker in the world. 'I believe Fernando has had no rival in Europe this season,' said Arbeloa in an interview with the Liverpool club website. 'Cristiano Ronaldo is more of a midfielder than anything else, but there is no striker who can get near Fernando. He has been the best in Europe and I am not saying that just because of his numbers; I say it because of his importance to the team. He took Liverpool to the semi-finals of the Champions League, scoring against Inter, Arsenal and Chelsea. He is always there.

'We [Spain] need to take advantage of Fernando like we have been doing at Liverpool. I have noticed that at Liverpool we have been able to make the most of Torres' qualities. When he gets away from his marker, we send the ball forward without doubting it.

'In Spain, there is more possession. I think if we risk those long balls for Fernando we can achieve the ideal mix. At Liverpool, we play very differently to how they play in Spain. In England, the football is more physical, with more contact and fight. That can only help the national team because we will have the same technically good players, but they are also used to more physical play and contact. You can see it at Liverpool. We have players with a lot of quality like Xabi Alonso and Torres, and they don't shy away from the physical contact. They are very good players, but they fight for every ball. That makes us [Spain] more complete. There is youth and experience, and, above all, good football. Why not this time?'

Alonso also felt Spain had an edge over their rivals with El Niño in the line-up. He said, 'The way we play with Spain is different to the way we play with Liverpool, but I think he is quite confident in himself. Whenever he gets the ball we think that something might happen. He has scored so many goals and hopefully he will continue this run in the Euros.

'Even the more optimistic [supporters] could be surprised at how easily he settled at Liverpool because of the way he has performed. He has been so confident on the pitch and in front of goal and that is great news for Liverpool and Spain. And, obviously, it is hard but once he learns a few more things he will be even better.'

And, just like Arbeloa, Alonso saw no reason why this should not be the year that Spain finally ended their long wait for a major trophy. 'There is no clear reason, but it's clear we have under-achieved [in the past],' he added. 'Each tournament is a great chance for us to try and prove that we can perform and be positive in a final tournament. Because of that, we have faith in ourselves and we will strive to reach the level we expect and want to reach.'

With a successful season at Liverpool behind him, and team-mates and opponents alike singing his praises, it was little wonder that Fernando approached the tournament full of confidence. But, for all his personal glory in his first year at Anfield, he had not won a trophy, and that was something he was desperate to put right. 'I have a lot of confidence following this season, but I am desperate to finish with a title,' he said. 'It would be a fantastic achievement for Spain and one which I think we are capable of.'

Torres knew, though, that, if he was to continue displaying the same rich vein of form for his country that he had done for his club, he would need to adapt his game accordingly. He told a media conference ahead of Spain's pre-tournament warm-up clash with the USA, 'It is obvious that the football is different from the Premier League, but those of us who come back from abroad need to adapt to the national team. In my case, I am the one that needs to adapt myself to the way the team plays and not the other way round. If this team is united and works as a unit, we can achieve great things.

'It is all the same to me because the national team has a definite system and it works well with one striker or two. It is much easier to adapt to playing alongside great players, like David Villa, and the quality that comes from midfield. This team likes to dominate the ball and is very offensive and, therefore, it is obvious that the defence will suffer more. But Spain has a good defence and we have shown that.

'I hope that it is Spain's European Championship, not just one player's. Everyone has to contribute to what we have up front and in defence because if we do that we will be able to achieve our aim. We are all here to give our bit for the cause, and to build a good team. We all defend and attack together, so the responsibilities and demands do not fall on just one person's shoulders; they are shared by everybody.'

An ankle injury had kept Torres out of training in the build-up to the game against the USA, but he was confident there would be no lasting problems and that he would be fully fit, both for Spain's final friendly and also for the tournament itself. He insisted, 'My ankle is fine. It was just one of those things that could happen in a training match, but it is getting better and better. I don't think that I am going to have any problems playing [against America]. It is up to the manager to decide, but the most important thing is to be ready for the European Championship.'

Torres was indeed fit enough to start against the USA, playing the first half of a match they won 1–0 with a goal from Xavi, a decent climax to their preparations for Euro 2008. Now, though, the real business was about to begin.

But Fernando was keen to play down talk of his side being the favourites to lift the trophy, and felt it was an added burden the squad could do without. He told Spanish journalist Guillem Balague, 'I don't believe [the expectations of the country] are false, but they are unnecessary. The favourites tag doesn't suit us – we're not. The favourite is a team like Italy that has just won the World Cup; or France, runners-up at the World Cup and European Champions I don't know how many times. It's all the rage to say that we are going to win and it seems like we've already been labelled as having almost won it. They're counting on us, and they use these terms to generate hope, but, at the end of the day, that gets confused with an obligation.

'Just imagine, if we reach the semi-finals, we'll have bettered many generations of the national team... teams as famous, or even more so, than ourselves. We want to win and I believe that we have a chance, with some very useful players. This creates unnecessary expectations and if this tournament doesn't turn out well, it gives the impression that everything we've achieved has been for nothing. And it's not like that. We've been through some bad times before reaching Austria, but we came through and, if things go badly, we'll come through again. But I can assure you, we do not need these false expectations.'

But if those words seemed to suggest that Spain would once more wilt under the pressures of delivering on the big stage, those fears were surely dispelled in their opening game against Russia. And they were dispelled in emphatic fashion.

The Russians were expected to provide a real test of Spain's credentials but they were ruthlessly brushed aside as Aragones' side displayed a genuine confidence in their play, running out convincing 4–1 winners. Torres was not among the scorers, with the personal glory going to his strike partner David Villa, who netted a hat-trick. But the Valencia man was quick to pay tribute to the part his team-mate had played in helping him score his treble, even though by the time he scored his third goal Torres had been replaced by Cesc Fabregas, who, in turn, added the fourth goal in the dying seconds.

But, after completing his hat-trick, it was Torres to whom Villa raced to celebrate his milestone. He said, 'I wanted to dedicate that third one to him because I owed him something for the first two. He made the first one and his run opened up the space for [Andres] Iniesta to make a pass for me to score the second.'

And coach Aragones also praised the part Fernando had played in the win, even though he had withdrawn him with just nine minutes of the second half played, a decision the striker was clearly unhappy with. 'I understand why the player is angry and I am behind him, but it is important to correct these things afterwards,' said the Spanish boss. 'They are things which stay in the dressing room but things won't stay like that, we won't let things like that fester. I understand that a player gets angry when he is substituted, it has happened to me, but the atmosphere in the team is extraordinary.

'There was no injury whatsoever. Torres has had a long, tough season and he will be a very important player for us [during the rest of the tournament]. But at that point we needed more strength in the centre of midfield. He was a very important player in helping Villa score the first goal and he made it tough for our opponents.'

With Sweden beating the reigning champions Greece 2-0 in their first match in the group, Spain knew that a victory over the Swedes in their second game would ensure their qualification for the quarter-finals. But no one in the camp was getting too carried away just yet. Torres told Spanish newspaper *Publico*, 'It is a good sign [that we started so well against Russia], but we have to learn from before – celebrate the victory a little, move on, and then turn our attentions to Sweden. The key is to continue how we are playing.

'We also have to remember what happened at the previous World Cup, because there are several teams out there who will punish any mistake you might make. It's good that there is enthusiasm, but not euphoria. Before the European Championship had kicked off, we heard all kind of stories, we were going to get knocked out at the quarter-final stage, or we were going to win the tournament. You hear so many things, but the conclusion we reached was that even we did not know how far we can go. Maybe all we need is to believe that we can actually do it. Euphoria leads you to believe that you are better than everyone, and the fact is that we are not.

'Right now we want to win. The anxiety and tension grows the more you progress. The tension, though, is not just felt by the players, it's all around. Come the quarter-finals, where we normally slip up, we will no doubt be anxious for the victory. I hope that we can avoid all the anxiety and tension in the run-up to "that" game, but I have been there before and we all realise that the last eight will be tough.

'We have to be convinced of winning, but also at the same time have our feet firmly on the ground. Look at what happened at the last World Cup; we were sure that we were going to win, but our belief turned into over-confidence. Maybe the goal we conceded late on versus Russia could well be a warning that we took our foot off the pedal. The game looked dead and buried, we relaxed a little too much, and they went and scored from a corner. We have to learn from those situations.'

Torres was also keen to down-play any suggestions of a rift between himself and Aragones following his substitution against the Russians. 'I don't know [why I was taken off], that is really a question for the boss,' he added. 'I play to win, to score, and to try and play as many minutes as possible. It is not up to me, though, but I will just have to try and play better so that it does not happen to me again.

'There is no problem. I have spoken to the coach and know it was just another change. I have no problems with him. It seems a shame that so much importance has been placed on this when Spain won 4–1. The rules of the dressing room, that Luis taught me when I was

16, are those that have worked for me now and what is said in the dressing room stays there. I would never make a rude gesture to a coach and the squad are completely behind him.'

But, although his substitution undoubtedly disappointed him, the reaction of Villa when he scored his third goal, and his subsequent dedication of it to Fernando, thrilled the Liverpool striker. He continued, 'Sometimes things don't go as well as you would like out there [on the pitch], or maybe you just don't get on the score sheet. But we strikers know how much work has to be put in up front, and although you can never know exactly what is going through someone's head, we appreciate our team-mates and their contribution.

'I have been on the other side of the fence, and have had colleagues run themselves into the ground so that I can score, and they never get a mention; but I have dedicated goals to them. All these factors show just what a great person Villa is.'

Spain were keen not to allow tales of supposed rifts to overshadow their preparations for the next game against Sweden. And, for their part, the Swedes were well aware of how tough an opponent Spain would be, with one player in particular needing no introduction to their danger man. Former Aston Villa defender Olaf Mellberg knew all about Spain's qualities, with Torres a threat he picked out for special mention.

'Fernando Torres is a world-class striker and you can't give him any time on the ball,' said the Juventus star. 'I played against Torres, Alonso and Reina in the Premier League last season, but I think they will play differently when we meet at Euro 2008. International football is very different to club football, so I think Spain will play a very different style of football to Liverpool. Spain are really good from set pieces – they have lots of players who can score from free-kicks and crosses. A lot of people think Spain can win Euro 2008.'

The match between the two in Innsbruck was certainly a tense affair, but it was Spain who were celebrating at the end as they clinched their place in the knockout stages. Torres opened the scoring with his first goal of the tournament, only to see his effort cancelled out by Zlatan Ibrahimovic. But, just as the game seemed destined to finish as a draw, Villa struck two minutes into injury time to confirm Spain's place in the last eight.

Aragones felt it was a victory his side deserved. He said, 'I think we were the better side, particularly in the second half. You could see Sweden were really very tired and we had the chances. The team played better when we managed to get the ball. I have lots of respect for Sweden, they're a good team who play long balls, but they play them well.

'We also played too many long passes because we have the speed of Torres. When they stole the ball, they really came back at us and it's hard to hold people who are 20cm taller than you. Sweden made us work very hard, but we had more of the ball and managed to create a couple of good chances. We were fortunate to have Villa, who scored a goal which was nearly impossible. You look at it from the outside and you say "How did he manage to score that?"

'You always have to believe in luck, even knowing the difficulties you have in games and that other teams play well. My celebration isn't very usual for me, but I saw the bench and it's important for a coach to see how people react to a goal there. I'm not a man who celebrates so it was unusual for me but the goal was so late. The beautiful thing was the way the players on the team went to those on the bench to celebrate together.'

And Torres was also satisfied after opening his goal account for the finals and seeing Spain safely negotiate the group phase with a game to spare. 'I'm pleased with this victory,' he said. 'My first goal? I remain calm – that's always been the case. I managed an important goal, like that of Villa, and now we've qualified. To win this type of competition one must know how to suffer, and we are a team that knows how to suffer. The key is to read games, because they won't all be as easy as the Russia encounter.'

Swedish star Mellberg, meanwhile, who had been so generous in his praise of Torres before the game, was even more so afterwards, revealing that he felt Spain had the striking power to lift the trophy. He said, 'Torres and Villa can win the tournament for Spain. They showed against us they can be under pressure, but have the strikers to do the job if they get a breakaway. That's all about confidence. When you've scored a few goals you've got that in the back of your head and you know that when you get the chance you can take it. That's their quality.

'Even though Spain had a lot of possession and dominated the game they struggled to create those really, really big chances. As a defender, you've got to be really aware and I thought we coped pretty well in the last third. But that's the way it is with really good strikers. They get one chance and they punish you.'

With qualification for the quarter-finals assured, Aragones chose to change his entire team for the final group game against the Greeks. It was testimony to the quality of the squad that the second string still managed to win that game 2–1, thanks to first international goals from Ruben de la Red and Daniel Guiza. That win suggested Spain had the strength in depth to win the tournament but, as Aragones faced up to the prospect of a last-eight showdown with world champions Italy, he knew his team still had a lot to prove. 'Let's hope we have enough quality to win in the quarter-finals,' he said. 'In the second half [against Greece], the effort from my players showed that they are in great shape physically. We didn't have the tempo we needed in the first half, we were playing at Greece's rhythm, but in the second half we played as well as we have played. We had five or six chances and could have scored more goals. We know we face a great opponent [in Italy]. It's going to be difficult but they probably think the same about us.

'Obviously, we are facing the world champions – the four-times world champions – so perhaps it is the most difficult of the quarter-finals but any tie at this stage is going to involve a strong team, and in the semi-finals even more so. All of the teams who have qualified have rested players because the tournament schedule is compressed into a few days and this means that players have got to be able to recuperate. The only thing we need now is a positive attitude. We have to forget it is Italy or whoever and think about winning – that's it. What's important is positive thinking and, with that, we will get there.'

The Spanish players knew the game against Italy would, without doubt, represent their toughest test of the tournament so far, even though the Italians had been less than impressive in the group stages. Torres even went so far as to suggest that the Azzurri were favourites. He said, 'Italy won the last World Cup and you don't achieve that by accident. They are a team we should respect and, given their past record, they are the favourites. But, although they may be favourites on paper, we have absolutely no fear of them. We beat them in a recent friendly and now we've got the chance to do the same in a competitive game.

'Spain are playing well, we are winning easily and we have a lot of alternatives. We expect to have the ball for long periods against Italy but we will have to be patient against them. They haven't been brilliant in the group but it was the same story at the World Cup and they ended up winning it. In the group, you can afford to have a bad day, but if that happens now you go home.'

Dutch star Dirk Kuyt, meanwhile, whose own Euro 2008 hopes had been ended in his country's last-eight clash with Russia, was tipping Torres and Villa to be the deadly double-act to gun down the Italians. 'We already know how good a player Fernando is,' said Kuyt. 'He showed it this season at Liverpool and it's not a surprise he is doing it in the Euros as well for Spain. He's one of the most important players for Spain and perhaps even the most important. Maybe Villa has scored the most goals in the Spanish team and is getting all the headlines but I think Fernando is the important one because he's so quick and has such great ability. He deserves all the credit as far as I'm concerned.'

The Italians, unsurprisingly, were also extremely wary of the threat posed by Spain's twin terrors of Torres and Villa. Cannavaro, who had singled out Torres as a danger man before the tournament started, warned his countrymen they would be facing the best pairing in the world. The Real Madrid defender had been ruled out of the tournament with injury before it started, but had kept a keen eye on proceedings and he insisted, 'These two [Torres and Villa] are the best partnership of any country in the world. They are so good they only need one chance to score two goals! They are different types of players as well, so we will have to be so careful. I'm glad we didn't have to play them in the World Cup.'

That endorsement was echoed by Christian Panucci, one of the men who would have the task of shackling the dynamic duo to try to preserve Italy's place in the tournament. But he warned that reputations would count for nothing come kick-off in Vienna. He said, 'Torres and Villa are strong, that's obvious. But [Karim] Benzema and [Thierry] Henry were supposed to be a strong strike force but look what happened there [when Italy beat France in the group stage]. Me and [Giorgio] Chiellini are doing really well at the back and I think he will be one of the best defenders in the world very soon.'

But, while Panucci remained confident of triumphing, his club manager at Roma, Luciano Spalletti, was less sure about his country's chances of halting Spain's golden boys. 'Italy need to be careful on the wings and they need to watch out for Fernando Torres and David Villa,' he said. 'Those two strikers are fast and excellent and it's fundamental that Italy are compact. We have to be ready and try and intercept the balls going towards Villa's feet. We also have to watch Torres' runs as well. Aragones has some great young players at his disposal and he is using them very well.'

It was Villa who had so far grabbed the lion's share of the headlines because of his goals, but Italian midfielder Mauro Camoranesi had no doubts who his side had to be most afraid of – Fernando Torres. He insisted, 'It will not be a battle of the individuals, but rather two excellent teams, as Spain are not only Villa. In fact, if I have to be perfectly honest with my own personal opinion here, I think Torres is a better and more complete forward than his team-mate.'

For all the plaudits heaped upon Torres and Villa before the game, however, and indeed on the free-flowing Spanish side as a whole, they were unable to break down a stubborn Italian rearguard when the action got under way. The Italians ceded the vast majority of possession to their rivals but defended like Italian teams of old and blunted everything the Spanish could throw at them, the result being that, at the end of 90 minutes plus extra-time, the quarter-final would be decided on a penalty shoot-out. And it was then that the weight of history must have come crashing down on the shoulders of the Spanish players.

The ability of Spanish sides to cope with the occasion on the biggest stage had long been questioned given their failures in previous World Cups and European Championships. Now, if they were to prevail, they would have to exorcise another ghost.

Remarkably, Spain had been beaten three times on penalties at the quarter-final stages of major tournaments – with all three defeats occurring on the same date, 22 June. In 1986, they lost to Belgium at the World Cup finals in Mexico. Ten years later, at Euro '96, the host nation England were their conquerors. And then, in

2002, their World Cup dreams were ended once again, this time by co-hosts South Korea.

And, as if the footballing gods were mocking them, here they were again, on 22 June 2008, facing another trial from 12 yards with a place in the semi-finals at stake. Add to that the fact that Spain had not beaten Italy in a major tournament since the 1920 Olympics, and a strong case could be made for Italy to be the overwhelming favourites at this stage.

But what is history if it is not for rewriting? And Spain confounded their critics by coming through the high-pressure lottery of the shoot-out, with goalkeeper Iker Casillas the hero. He made saves to deny Daniele De Rossi and Antonio Di Natale, while only Daniel Guiza failed for the Spanish as they clinched a 4–2 victory to seal a semi-final date with Russia.

It was a result that delighted Aragones, although he made it clear that he did not feel the job had been done merely by reaching the final four. He said, 'We won through, but we have only won a small battle. I think we deserved to win. We didn't play great, but nor did Italy. We should have used more pace. The tempo was rather slow and if we'd played the ball quicker we'd have created more chances. We were a little fresher, but lacked speed with the ball to carry it quicker and at times we lost possession. We got into the Italian lines but couldn't complete our link play. We lost quite a bit of possession, though the team was in a good physical shape and Italy could only use the high ball against us.

'I'm doing my job – as a coach I'm here to win. For Spain, it's important. We have struggled to get past the quarters before but now we've done that so let's see if we can get to the final. I'm not depressed when I lose, I'm not euphoric when I win. I'm happy for my country, happy for my players and also for me – this is my profession.

'This team wants to go to the final and win. It's now more difficult [against Russia] than at the beginning [of the tournament]. This is a great time for Russian football, because at this stage of their season they are at their peak. Many say we've beaten them before so it will be easy but it's much more complicated.'

But, while Aragones reacted to the victory over Italy in typically deadpan fashion, his players were far more excited about what they had achieved. 'I'm enjoying this victory,' said a beaming Torres. 'I think we all must look back at the harder moments to realise how important this is. This is the most beautiful time I've ever experienced with the Spanish team. We are euphoric. It was a very difficult game because of our opponents and because of the curse of the quarter-finals and we knew that it was going to be very important for the morale of the team.

'This moment is not only great for our group of 23 players, nor just for our generation – this moment is legendary for several generations. All of Spain has to feel part of this moment, not only us. We are very fortunate to be here now.'

And Fernando revealed he was always confident in Casillas when it came to spot-kicks, even though he was forced to watch the action from the side of the pitch having again been substituted during the game. He added, 'Iker [Casillas] has done very well because not only has he done well in the penalties, but he also saved a very clear scoring chance during the game. There is little you can say about Casillas... we all know the goalkeeper that we have. I was confident in Iker. These games are decided by the smallest details and he has shown that he is the best.'

The dramatic shoot-out victory over Italy set up a second meeting in as many weeks with Russia, whom Spain had beaten so convincingly in their opening game of the tournament. Not that they were taking their place in the final for granted. 'This game against Russia will be very different to the first game,' insisted Fernando. 'They are a team who are showing a great level, and are a team that have proved to be in top form, but, if we have beaten them once, I am sure that we can beat them again.'

Midfielder Xavi Hernandez, meanwhile, admitted that the Spaniards had fortune on their side in the first game [against Russia] and that they needed to guard against complacency in Vienna. He said, 'The boss has already pointed it out so I'm not shy of admitting that we had a couple of moments of luck at the beginning of our 4–1 win over Russia in the first match. They hit the post, we scored right on half-time and that blow to their rhythm helped us impose our game. Now they're facing us again with massively more self-belief and confidence thanks to three wins, but also the fact that they've been better than their opponents in each of their matches since. I'm sure that this semi will be totally different from the first match for these reasons and the key will not only be who has the better possession but how that team uses it.

'Getting through the quarter-finals was joyful and historic, but not nearly enough. We have to take this opportunity now, get through the semi-final and then win the entire tournament. We've had that as our aim for months and we've believed in it. You can feel the momentum. Not only are we playing well but cleverly, too, and we are getting the little breaks like Russia hitting the post and Iker saving two penalties. I know we have a winning mentality and if we are properly mentally prepared for beating Russia then we'll achieve it.'

And achieve it they did, in fine style, as goals from Xavi, Daniel Guiza and David Silva sealed an emphatic 3–0 win and booked Spain a place in the final against Germany and the chance to end 44 years of disappointment for a country that shares a collective passion for football. It would be a fitting finale for Aragones, who was set to leave his post as Spain's national coach at the end of the finals to take charge of Turkish side Fenerbahçe.

He said, 'We started the match by playing the kind of football that Russia like – long passes and so on – but when we started touching the ball [more] we were more complete, both attacking and defending. We scored three goals and in a semi-final that's very difficult indeed. We talked it over at half-time and said we had to quicken the pace because we knew if we scored we would hurt them badly, and that's what happened. When Russia tried to attack we were very good, too, we kept the ball well.'

The only black mark for the Spanish on a night of wild celebration was an injury to the tournament's leading scorer, David Villa, which threatened to rule him out of the final. 'Villa is injured and I don't know whether he'll play in the final,' added Aragones. 'But in any case we played better with one forward than two. It's fantastic the way we're playing. It's better for numbers, players and pressing – and that's how you get Xavi to score. The point is to make them feel free.

'I'm not an extrovert but I feel very happy inside. I'm very happy inside for myself, my players, the fans and even my family. I'm not an expressive person, I don't show my feelings so much. I don't celebrate too much when we win or get too depressed when we lose but I'm very happy for the players.

'They deserve to be champions, but we still have a tough game ahead against Germany. When we came to the tournament we knew we had a good team and could go very far and people have learned. We've had a tough time in some matches but we've always believed in ourselves and we have a great team.'

As for Torres, while he was thrilled at making his first major final, he had no intention of merely making up the numbers in the tournament's finale. All he cared about was coming out on top. 'It's nice to be in the final, but no one remembers the runners-up,' he insisted. 'We want to be champions so everyone talks about us at least for the next four years until the next European Championship. I hope the best is still to come. It's a big success that Spain is in the final, but we're not settling for that – we want to be champions.'

Aragones, meanwhile, was hoping that the almost siege mentality he had instilled in his squad in the face of widespread criticism during those dark early days of the qualification stages would serve them well against the Germans. 'I'm happy to have a group that believes in me and the way we work,' he said. 'We've gone through difficult periods and I've gone through the worst of those times but that brought us together. When you are united good things happen. At the start when we were heavily criticised the players saw I worked even harder and they supported me. They understood I was on the right path. I have seen great teams with great players but if you don't have a good atmosphere you cannot win. The great atmosphere in this squad has helped us reach the final. Above all we're a group. We understand if we work together we can win.

'I fear some things [about Germany]. For example, their strength in the air, their incredible speed and their physical strength. And, of course, their fast counter-attacks, but we'll have to tackle those. We have our own way of playing. It has been the same for the past four years and we will continue the same way. We're not good when we adapt our play. We must follow our way to win.

'I believe my team will win. Of course, I have dreamed [of winning], but I dreamed of the World Cup and it didn't happen. Now I'm dreaming of the European Championship and it is possible. But coaches are always dreaming, because they want to win every game. Winning by playing good football is even better.'

As it was, Aragones' fears proved unfounded and his dreams came true as Spain clinched the title with a 1–0 win over Germany. Although the final scoreline suggested a narrow victory, the Spanish performance was an absolute masterclass as they totally dominated their much-decorated opponents. That they had only one goal to show for their superiority was a shame, but the goal itself was worthy of winning any match.

Playing up front on his own in the absence of the sidelined Villa, Torres terrorised the German defence throughout. He had already hit the post with a header before he provided the game's decisive finish in the 33rd minute, outmuscling and outpacing full-back Philip

Lahm to reach Xavi's through ball before clipping his shot over the advancing Jens Lehmann and into the net.

His reward for his magnificent performance, aside from the goal of course, was being named as the official UEFA Man of the Match for the final. He had been just three months old the last time Spain had played in a major final in 1984 and, perhaps fittingly, the man who had done so much to end their dream in that final 24 years previously, former French captain Michel Platini, was on hand this time in his role as UEFA President to hand over the trophy.

And so at the end of a splendid 90 minutes by his team, and at the conclusion of two years' hard work following their World Cup disappointment in Germany, it was an emotional Aragones who faced the media after the game in his final press conference as his country's coach.

He said, 'We have put together a group that plays well, that keeps the ball and mixes their passes very well and that is difficult to stop. We work hard together, those that play more and those that play slightly less, and we've managed to get there. This is a happy day for Spain – we've won this tournament in style and we're very happy. Now we will start expecting to win on this sort of stage. Many people will look at this Spain team because it has been a model for playing football. I think all football lovers want people to make good combinations, to get into the penalty area and to score goals.

'At the beginning, I said that, if we managed this squad well, we would be champions. The team just thought I was trying to give them confidence. I just hope Spain carry on in this way and have many more victories.

198

'I am delighted. I usually don't show what I feel, but I'm full inside. I don't get very emotional but there were moments out there from some of my players that filled me with emotion. I'm like that – I don't show it but I'm so full of feelings. That's my way of showing it – other people might be more expressive.'

And Aragones reserved special praise for his team's match-winner against the Germans. He added, 'Fernando Torres is a great player for Liverpool and for Spain. He can do anything. Why? He has such extraordinary speed and he knows how to dribble at pace. He is so young and could learn to do anything. He could be one of the best players in the world, no doubt.'

For Fernando himself, success in the final was a realisation of one of his greatest ambitions and he was overwhelmed by what he and his team-mates had achieved. 'It's a dream come true,' he said. 'At last, justice has been done because the team that played the best football won the tournament. I feel a tremendous joy. It still hasn't sunk in what we've achieved. This is my first title and I hope it's the first of many. We are used to watching finals on television, but today we were here and we won. The team that has played the best football in the tournament has won the title and now we have a place in European football history. It's our first title [together] and we hope it will be the first of many. We've still got the World Cup to come, we have to be ambitious.'

Victory at Euro 2008 capped a memorable 12 months for Torres but he insisted it was just the start as he immediately set his sights on winning more trophies. 'It has been a fantastic season for me with a great end with Spain,' he said. 'I have to keep going now. I want to win more titles. I want to be the most important player in Europe and in the world.'

And he also had a special word of recognition for those in England who had played their own part in helping him achieve success with his country. He added, 'I would like to thank all the staff and players at Liverpool for their support during Euro 2008 because it makes a real difference when you know you have the backing of the people of your club. Because of this they share in our success.

'I have had a wonderful first season at Anfield and the goals I scored for Liverpool gave me the confidence and belief I needed for the Euros. Again, I would like to thank Rafa Benitez and his staff because I have improved as a player thanks to them.

'But it isn't just the people at the club who have helped me, it is also the supporters and the people of the city. From the moment I first came to Liverpool, I have been made to feel welcome and that is why I am able to enjoy my football so much. It is incredible because the Liverpool fans have given me so much support and I know that they have even been supporting Spain. This is something I will never forget and I thank everyone for that. Now I am looking forward to competing for trophies with the Reds because I know that means so much to the club and the fans.'

7

BACK WITH
THE REDS

It's doubtful that a comic-book scriptwriter could have penned a more memorable 12 months for Fernando Torres than those he had just enjoyed. A record-breaking transfer to Liverpool, a stunning first season in the Premier League and a first major trophy at Euro 2008 – it would be fair to say that life was treating him pretty well.

Even so, doubts still remained. Could he perform as well again for a second successive season? Would Premier League defenders now be ready for him? How would he cope after the highs of a sensational summer with Spain?

All of those questions were waiting to be answered, but the player himself could not wait to get started as he prepared for a second season at Anfield. 'I am very excited about the new season. After a first year in England that I consider to be very positive, it's now important for me to consolidate and to continue helping the team do well,' he said in an interview with *FootballPunk* magazine. 'We will do our best [to win a trophy this season]. It won't be easy because we have a lot of rivals, but we have to do well in the key moments and believe in ourselves. My dream is to win a title with Liverpool.

'I have been very fortunate with Spain and enjoyed the best moment of my sporting life in the summer when we won Euro 2008. So I know what it feels like to win a big trophy. Now I want to experience this feeling with Liverpool. The sad part last year was that we didn't win any trophies. We were just one step away from reaching the Champions League final and that still feels like a nail in my heart. I have never been through something like that. Never. So this year I want to go all the way to the end.'

There was no doubt that Torres, after such a great debut campaign in England, would be a marked man in the Premier League in the months to come. But a former Anfield legend was backing him to shine once more, even though he felt the forthcoming challenges might be even greater than those he had already overcome. Ian Rush told *Football2009* magazine, 'I expect it to be tougher for him next season but, from what we've already seen, we know he will be a success again. Opposition players tried every trick in the book in an attempt to put him off his stride last season. They tried to outmuscle him and kick him out of the game but he always came back and just got on with his game. That's what I like most about him.

'The English game is played at 100mph, much quicker than in Spain and it's much more physical. But Torres has just got on with it and has proven he is up to it by scoring goal after goal. As a striker, you always look to try and better yourself each season. In that sense, as long as he equals what he did last year, he'll be happy. He'll be looking to do that and I hope he can. But the main thing is that the team is successful and winning things. I'm sure he'd swap ten or 15 goals for Liverpool to win a trophy.'

Rush, of course, knew very well what it was like to move to a foreign country with a big price tag on your head and fully appreciated the challenges a transfer like that entailed. He scored 139 goals in 224 Liverpool appearances between 1980 and 1987 before an unhappy year in Italy with Juventus. And he admitted he was shocked by how quickly Torres had adapted to a new style of football, not to mention a whole new culture. 'I am surprised that he did so well, so soon,' continued the striker, who scored a further 90 goals in a red shirt following his return from Serie A. 'For someone to score that amount of goals in his first season is incredible. His goals-to-games ratio in Spain wasn't actually as good as it could have been. Looking at his record there, I was thinking that if he got 20 or so goals in total last season that would have been considered a success. But to get 30-plus was something I hadn't thought about or expected from him. Torres is something special.'

Whether or not the unassuming Spaniard would use the word 'special' to describe himself is open to debate, but where he did agree with Rush was in the Welshman's assessment of the surprise factor surrounding his first year in England. 'I went to the Premier League thinking it might take a year or so to adapt to a new life and a new style of play before getting near my personal best. So scoring 33 goals in one season was beyond my dreams because my record at Atletico Madrid was 21,' he continued in *FootballPunk*. 'When I signed for Liverpool, I said that one of my main targets was to increase my average goals-per-season ratio and I have done that. To be among the top three goalscorers in the Premier League in my debut year was unthinkable just a year ago. Things went really well. Now I want that to continue in the new season.'

And he admitted that he would not get carried away after winning Euro 2008, nor would his head be turned by the people now hailing him as the best centre-forward in the world. He added, 'Spain's victory [at Euro 2008] has not turned me crazy. I am the same person I was before, with my feet firmly on the ground. I know now that everyone will look at me in more detail and watch closely what I do, but I have to continue down the same road of hard work and sacrifice to do well with Liverpool.

'I don't think I am the best centre-forward in the world – I have a lot to learn yet and a lot to win yet. Obviously, that is my goal as a professional, but right now I don't think about that or about winning a golden ball or being named the best player in the world. I'm not thinking of individual prizes. I only want to start the season well with Liverpool and to have the options to win titles this season.'

In a bid to achieve that long-awaited title success, manager Benitez had a special 'welcome home' gift for Torres when he returned to pre-season training following an extended break after Euro 2008 – a new strike partner. With much of the focus throughout the summer having been on Liverpool's protracted and ultimately unsuccessful pursuit of Aston Villa midfield star Gareth Barry, very few people could have expected the big signing they actually did make. It was Tottenham captain Robbie Keane who, instead, arrived at Anfield for a fee of £20m to form a new-look front two with Torres that Benitez hoped would prove to be a lethal combination.

He told the club's website, 'We were looking for a player with game intelligence and good movement who could play alongside Torres. He can play with Torres up front and also on the right. We know he has always been a Liverpool fan, and we knew that he was a very good signing in terms of the commitment, the quality and the intelligence of the player. He is a player who can give to us a lot of goals – normally he gets about 15 each year. We were looking for the work rate he can give to us, the game intelligence and also the goals.

'He has experience in the Premier League and also all the reports of his personality and professionalism are fantastic. He can be a good example for the young players. I feel like he has enough experience in the game and that he has a very good mentality. He is very hungry, so everything is positive!'

The potential link-up with Keane was one that certainly appealed to Torres. He said, 'Robbie really wanted to come to us and you can already see he is going to bring us an enormous amount – hard work, goals and experience. He will bring the level of the team up a notch. Keane has a proven record and great mobility and versatility. He can play on the wing or a bit behind the striker. It is very good for the team to have a player who can get in between the opposition's midfield and defence and score goals.

'The tactical lay-out of the team, and whether or not we are going to play two up front, is down to Rafa Benitez. When he signed Keane I'm sure he had a very clear idea of where he wanted to play him. But he is very adaptable. He could fill a number of different roles!'

The first opportunity for Keane and Torres to play together came at the end of July in a friendly away to Villarreal, but Benitez resisted the opportunity to pair them in attack, preferring instead to give Keane the first 45 minutes only, before introducing Torres as a substitute with just 20 minutes remaining. Even so, Keane had seen enough in training to believe that he and Torres could form a dangerous combination.

'I didn't get the chance to partner Fernando this time, but I am looking forward to it when it does happen,' he told the club's website after the Villarreal match. 'I'm settling in just fine and it was good to get 45 minutes under my belt with my new team-mates. I know I did not get to play alongside Fernando but I am sure any partnership will work well, but only time will tell. He's a tremendous player and it will be great to play up front alongside him. But it is up to the pair of us to make it work.'

Torres and Keane might have been kept apart for the trip to Villarreal but, just a few days later in Glasgow, Reds' fans got their first chance to see the pair in action as they started up front together against Rangers. They played only the first 45 minutes before Torres made way for another new signing, David Ngog, but in that first half there were plenty of signs of encouragement that the duo could prove to have a great understanding.

Certainly, things improved for the team as a whole at Ibrox after a less than impressive pre-season in front of goal thus far. In the five previous friendlies against Tranmere, Lucerne, Wisla Krajkow, Hertha Berlin and Villarreal, they had scored just four goals. Against Rangers, they scored that many in 90 minutes.

Perhaps unsurprisingly, it was Torres who led the way, opening the scoring after 23 minutes. And further goals after the break from Ngog, Yossi Benayoun and Xabi Alonso made it a thoroughly satisfying night's work for the team, and for the manager. Benitez enthused about what he had seen from his first-choice front two, saying, 'Both players [Torres and Keane] showed good movement, and their understanding with Steven Gerrard was good. With Yossi Benayoun and Dirk Kuyt both going inside it meant we had five offensive players who have good quality.

'Keane is a clever player who is working hard. He is very happy here. We will see a lot of good movement and a lot of goals. We have quality now and if we can keep the ball we will provide problems for any opposition.'

Of course, as would become apparent, Keane would have enough problems of his own at Liverpool, resulting in his transfer back to Tottenham in the January transfer window, but for now hopes were high.

Rangers manager Walter Smith was certainly full of praise for the Anfield outfit's new-look strike force and predicted that this could be the year the Reds finally sustained a long overdue title challenge. 'Torres and Keane are two very good players,' said the Ibrox boss. 'Liverpool will obviously benefit from that. It will maybe mean a change of emphasis in the way they play, but they have great players overall and, looking at them now, you'd say they have an opportunity this season to challenge for the title. I think they can push forward and improve on their top-four finishes in recent seasons and Torres and Keane could give them that little edge.'

Torres also felt his burgeoning partnership with Keane would reap dividends for the Reds in the months to come. 'Robbie's a fantastic player and an important player for us,' the Spaniard told liverpoolfc.tv. 'I hope he can score a lot of goals for Liverpool and that I can play alongside him many times. We've only been training together for a few days so it's not a lot of time, but the important thing for me is that he is always talking during games. The understanding between us and Steven Gerrard is important as well. He is the midfielder who is passing the ball to myself and Robbie and so the more training we do together the more good things we can do for Liverpool.'

Torres was also happy to open his goal account after the summer, but admitted he was still some way short of match fitness after his exertions in Austria and Switzerland. 'It was perfect to score my first goal because that's always important for strikers. I've only been training for one week and so it's understandable to feel tired. The idea is to arrive fit and ready for the start of the Premier League season. It was a fantastic summer for Spain but now my thoughts are with Liverpool. Hopefully we will win a trophy – I want to win the Premier League or the Champions League.'

Liverpool continued their pre-season preparations with another fine win, this time in Norway against Valerenga, whom they defeated 4-1, with Torres again finding the target, before their final pre-season match, and their only one at home, against Italian giants Lazio, a game they won 1-0. It meant Liverpool ended their pre-season campaign with five wins and three draws from their eight matches – more than satisfactory. But it was the potential of the

Torres–Keane partnership that had the fans most excited. And it was excitement the two players themselves were feeling. Keane told the official club magazine, 'I think Torres will get better this year, which is great news for Liverpool and has got to be a worry for the rest of the division. For me, Torres has just got to be about the best striker in the world at the moment. You saw how good he was at the European Championship, and I'm sure scoring the winning goal in the final will have done his confidence the world of good.

'I'm looking forward to playing alongside him – of course I am. Torres is the kind of striker that anyone would want to play alongside. He makes great runs, holds the ball up well to allow support to get around him and when he gets the chance in front of goal he's deadly.

'I can't wait for the real stuff to start and hopefully we'll work well together. I don't see any reason why we won't be a successful partnership but the manager's got a lot of options in attack so I'm really going to have to hit the ground running.'

Hitting the ground running is something Benitez would have been hoping all his team would do on their first competitive outing against Standard Liège in the Champions League third qualifying round. And he was certainly confident his strikers would do just that, hailing Torres and Keane as potentially the best pairing in Europe. 'I think they could be the best partnership in the Champions League,' he said. 'These two are top class. It would be better if they had played together for a long time but they're both clever players and they will have an even better understanding over time. I think they will be OK and can show their quality. In the time they have had together, they have played well and we have been scoring goals. They need time but we have confidence in them and I think we played well in the last game against Lazio.

'This pre-season was a bit different because we had players like Torres coming back late after Euro 2008 and then we signed Keane, too. It's not an ideal situation at this stage but hopefully it will be enough – the very least we will be looking for is an away goal [against Liège]. I have confidence in my players but you must always be careful of any team you come up against in Europe. I know Liège lost to St Etienne in a friendly but they also won the Belgian Super Cup recently so we need to be careful.

'We have been trying to learn a lot about Liège and have been watching the games they have been playing recently and, of course, analysing last season, too. We have some information. My staff have been watching games from last season but they have changed coach since then so to see them now is more important.

'Any top side competing in this competition must be aware of the quality of the teams involved. We must be focused in every game and make sure we do not make any mistakes. We know it's important to qualify every year and hopefully it will be the same this year.'

But the trip to last season's Belgian champions proved to be anything but plain sailing and Liverpool could count themselves fortunate to come away with a 0–0 draw. It could, in fact, have been much worse and could have derailed their European season before it had even got started. Fortunately for the Reds, however, goalkeeper Pepe Reina was in fine form and made a string of excellent saves, including one from Dante Bonfirm Costa's first-half penalty, to ensure the scoreline remained at 0–0 with the return leg at Anfield to come.

The lacklustre performance must have come as a total shock to Benitez and he admitted, 'We did not play well. The only positive thing you can take is that we didn't concede a goal. We know we have to win at Anfield and we have confidence we can. We will have had more games and more players available. There were a lot of things that we were not doing well and everyone is upset that it was a bad performance.'

Perhaps the only good news for Liverpool was that the first Premier League game of the season was just three days later, giving them an immediate chance to get the disappointment of the Liège performance out of their system. And they surely knew that a repeat of that below-par display against Sunderland at the Stadium of Light would see them return from the north-east without a point, with Roy Keane's side desperate to make a good start to the season and turn their home base into a fortress.

For long periods, it was an unimpressive performance by Liverpool but, just when it looked as though they would have to settle for a single point on the opening day, Torres struck with a magnificent 25-yard drive to seal victory with just seven minutes left on the clock. It was a terrific strike from a player whose confidence was clearly still sky-high following his summer exploits, and it came as no surprise to his team-mates. Defender Sami Hyypia said, 'It was a good finish from Fernando. I was just behind the shot and I could see exactly where it was going. It was a great strike and it gave the goalkeeper no chance. None of us were surprised that Fernando scored in that way because we have seen him do it before in games and he also does it in training. It's great for us that we have that kind of player in our team.'

In truth, it was Torres' only real contribution of note in a largely forgettable match, but all great strikers have the happy habit of popping up with a goal just when their side needs it most. That was certainly how the *Guardian* saw things in their report of the match, which read, 'Fabio Capello believes Fernando Torres is the best striker in the world and, although he did not look it here, he did sink Sunderland with a wonder goal seven minutes from time and that is all anyone can ask of a world-class striker.

'To the enviable talents fully displayed last season and in the European Championship in the summer can now be added the knack of appearing to sleepwalk through a game before bursting into life with one decisive moment. The match was petering out to a draw and Sunderland had no reason to suspect imminent danger when Torres collected Xabi Alonso's shrewd pass just outside the centre circle, took a couple of strides towards goal and shot past Craig Gordon from 25 yards out.'

It was, of course, simply the latest in a long line of match-winning performances by the Spaniard that once again left his manager thankful to have his star striker to call upon in times of trouble.

Benitez said, 'I think it was a difficult game in the first half. They controlled the game in the opening 45 minutes but didn't have clear chances, other than maybe one. We were a little under pressure but the second half was different. We were controlling it and the quality of our passing was much better. We had plenty of possession and were much better going forward. The difference at the end of the game was Torres. We know he can score these kinds of goals but the team as a whole needs to play well.'

Although the overall team performance may not have thrilled Benitez, winning was the main thing. If Liverpool were to make a challenge for the title, they simply had to start the season well and not allow the likes of Manchester United and Chelsea to open up an early lead. In Torres, they had a man they were confident would help prevent that, with Dirk Kuyt even going so far as to suggest that the Spanish star could play a role for the Reds as significant as that of Cristiano Ronaldo for Manchester United the season before. 'Can Fernando get the title for Liverpool as Ronaldo did last season? Why not? Of course they are different players, he [Ronaldo] comes in from the side but Fernando is a real striker. He has everything to be the best player this season,' Kuyt said in a press conference. 'There was nothing on when he got the ball [against Sunderland] but he scores a few goals like that. He is always looking for the target and, as soon as he gets space to shoot, he shoots and often scores.

'He is a megastar now but not only is he a great striker but also a great personality. He is just the same on the pitch, in the dressing room, outside the game. Off the pitch, he is just a normal guy, just one of us, but on the pitch he is different. He is something special.

'Fernando played wonderfully at the Euros as well and always when you need him he scores very important goals. He is a top-quality player and, for me, he is the best striker in the world. If you are speaking about a real striker, he is the pinnacle, he is everything... not only in normal games but, more often than not, in special games.

'His partnership with Robbie Keane is getting better and if you are good players like those two it does not need much time, they will get used to each other. It is just about feeling and I am sure the partnership will grow and grow.'

For his part, Torres was naturally delighted to open his Premier League account in the very first game of the new season. After scoring 33 goals in his debut season, he was obviously keen to get off the mark quickly once more. Not that he wasn't confident of repeating the previous term's success, particularly with the inside knowledge he was receiving. The source of this vital information was the club's goalkeeping coach, Xavi Valero. Fernando revealed, 'We've a Spanish goalkeeping coach and he has been a genius at telling me every week exactly what kind of task lies in front of me in the following match. Nobody has ever worked with me like this before. It's outstanding. Basically, I know days before the next game exactly the best way to finish a chance against the keeper I'm about to face. Xavi Valero tells me precisely what each keeper tends to do – stay big, go down early, if they have a preferred side they try to push you to. It's vital information. I've refined the way I take chances as a result.'

And, if that surveillance from Valero paid off in the next nine months as well as it had done during his first campaign at Anfield, Torres, and the club as a whole, could look forward to a successful season. That was certainly what he had in mind as he concentrated his efforts on ensuring that this would finally be Liverpool's year for domestic glory. He said, 'Our focus is on the Premier League and we know how important it is to win the Premier League for the fans. It has been too many years and we are focusing on that. It was important to start with a win after the not so very good game in the Champions League.'

Indeed, starting with a win was important, but equally important was backing that up with three points in their first home game of the season against Middlesbrough. But they came perilously close to failing to do so. Rafa Benitez had said before the start of the season that his players needed to learn to 'win ugly' and they certainly did just that against Gareth Southgate's vibrant Boro side. The visitors dominated for large sections of the game and, in truth, would have been deserving winners. They had taken the lead with 20 minutes remaining thanks to a terrific 25-yard drive from striker Mido and looked well on course to take three excellent points at Anfield.

And they remained on track for that until just four minutes before the end when Jamie Carragher, of all people, galloped into the penalty area and saw his shot deflected home via defender Emanuel Pogatez, who had absolutely no chance of getting out of the way of the path of the ball. And so it appeared that Liverpool had rescued a point right at the death, but better was to come for the home side when Steven Gerrard smashed home a fantastic winner in the fourth minute of injury time.

It was a cruel blow to Middlesbrough, although very few people inside the ground were complaining. However, Benitez admitted his side had been lucky. He said, 'A draw would have been OK [after Mido scored]. Obviously, I am really happy with the result – but not the performance. I haven't been for the last three games and clearly we can improve. The main thing is we are trying until the end. We are not playing well and winning, whereas last year we were playing well but not scoring or winning. We have six points and know if we play really well it will be difficult to stop us – we will be a threat for everyone.'

There was clearly no escaping the fact that Liverpool were not at the top of their form, or anywhere near it for that matter and, with the return against Standard Liège to come in midweek, they knew they had to raise their game. The Reds had been given a scare in Belgium and knew they could not afford any mistakes at Anfield. Failure to qualify for the Champions League was simply unthinkable, not just because of the riches on offer but also for the reputations of a high-class squad of players.

Jamie Carragher summed up the mood when he said, 'We haven't clicked yet, there is no hiding from that, and if we perform as we have done over the last few weeks it is going to be extremely difficult to beat Liège. We realise we have to step it up a level, but we have won two out of two and long may that continue, but we know we will improve. There is a lot of pressure when you play for Liverpool and I know what the headlines would have been had we lost to Middlesbrough – they would have said the title's over.

'I've been here long enough to know what it's like, so to reverse it and go top of the league shows what fine lines there are in football. I'm sure there would have been a lot of criticism of the players and the manager had we lost but we are top of the league and that's the difference. But it is too early in the season to say where we are as a team. The proof that we have improved will be there after several months.'

It was clear that, despite a 100 per cent start and top spot in the Premier League, nobody at Anfield was overly impressed with the opening couple of weeks of the season. But, with the return leg against Liège next on the horizon, Benitez was confident his side would improve. And on the eve of that match against the Belgians, with a place in the money-spinning group stage at stake, he insisted that his motivation was to win trophies, not simply to fill the club's coffers from lucrative European TV rights deals. 'The first thing for me is the silverware. I like to talk about trophies,' he insisted at a media briefing. 'After that comes money. You have to put both things together, but for me we are here to win titles. But the one thing we know is we need to win for different reasons. I am not thinking about losing.

'I spoke to my players and told them, if you win games and trophies, you will have more money. It's the same for the club. We know the money is really important but it won't make a difference now we are so close to the transfer window closing.

'We were lucky to leave Belgium with a 0–0 draw. We didn't play well and it was really disappointing for me. We know this [Liège team] is a good team. If they were to go through, it would be a fantastic achievement for them. We have to be confident. But we will need to score more than one goal, just in case. The Champions League is a massive competition and it will be fantastic to get into the group stages, but we are expected to do it. If you told me 100 times we had a game at Anfield to go through to the Champions League, I would say yes every time.'

And captain Gerrard was also in confident mood, believing that the first leg in Belgium would provide the incentive the Reds needed to ensure there would be no repeat of that sloppy display at home. He said, 'Sometimes you need the kick up the backside similar to the one we had against Liège. You don't want to go into the season a little bit complacent and no one could argue against the fact Liège were the better team on the night. It was certainly a wake-up call for us and the best thing about it was that we didn't get beaten. We're still in the tie and know we will play a lot better at Anfield. Liège will also find it more difficult.'

In fact, for all the bullish pre-match comments, Liverpool needed a solitary goal from Dirk Kuyt just two minutes from the end of extra-time to spare them the ignominy – and possibly the agony – of a penalty shoot-out against opponents they had been extremely confident of beating comfortably. It was worrying that a side that had been so impressive at the top of Europe's table for the past three years should stumble so uneasily over the line eventually to book their place in the group stages of the competition proper. It was clear to all, however, that if Liverpool were to once again challenge for the trophy there would need to be a vast improvement all round.

Not that Benitez was entirely unsatisfied. He said, 'We knew it could be difficult. From the first minute they played well and we knew they would play well on the counter-attack so we had to work really hard until the end. For me, the most positive thing is that we played a little bit better against a good team who are sharp and we scored at the end. That means that the team are working really hard.'

Unconvincing though the performance may have been, the end result was achieved – qualification for the group phase. It is an arena in which Liverpool have proved masterful in recent years. The Reds joined Premier League adversaries Arsenal, Chelsea and Manchester United in the pot of top seeds in the draw, but such was the strength of possible opponents that Liverpool knew they could find themselves in a group with the likes of Bayern Munich, Juventus, Roma, Porto or Atletico Madrid.

Jamie Carragher told the club's website, 'We're looking forward to the draw. It's always a great occasion to see who you get and we're guaranteed six games now. With our record over the last few years, we're confident that whoever we play we'll get through. The Champions League is about playing the best teams so I'm not looking to avoid anyone.'

In the end, the draw in Monaco paired Liverpool with Marseille, PSV Eindhoven and Atletico Madrid, meaning an emotional return to the Vicente Calderon for Torres – a trip 'home' he was relishing. 'It will be a very special occasion for me [to go back to Atletico] and I am sure that I am going to enjoy the experience,' he said on his official website. 'I hope that the fans give me a warm welcome, because Atletico gave me many things, but I also gave a lot to Atletico. I will understand that, as soon as the ball starts to roll, the fans will see me as a rival, but I will never be able to forget all the years I spent at the club.

'It's going to be an amazing feeling when I step out on to the Vicente Calderon pitch again and come face to face with old team-mates and friends. It's a complicated group, very difficult and every game will be a final. Olympique Marseille made life hard for us last year, beating us at Anfield and leaving us no option but to win at their ground to guarantee our qualification from the group. PSV Eindhoven are a hard-working side, and Atletico will be looking to impress on their return to European football. There can be no question, though – my wish is that both Liverpool and Atletico make the last 16.'

Before Torres and his team-mates could concentrate on Europe, however, there were domestic and international commitments to fulfil. Liverpool faced Aston Villa in their next Premier League game, their third of the campaign, before a two-week break for the start of the European nations' World Cup qualifying campaign.

For Torres, though, the two-week break would mean just that. The striker had to leave the field after just 30 minutes at Villa Park – in a game that finished 0–0 – following a hamstring pull and he was immediately withdrawn from the Spanish squad for their matches against Bosnia-Herzegovina and Armenia.

Fortunately for the Spanish, they did not miss Torres too much as they safely secured 1–0 and 4–0 home wins respectively to get their qualifying campaign off to the perfect start. Of more concern to Rafa Benitez and Liverpool was the fact that Torres now faced a race against time to be fit for the next Premier League match – a home meeting with arch rivals Manchester United. And, with Steven Gerrard also doubtful after missing England's opening World Cup qualifiers to undergo a groin operation, Benitez was contemplating the unhappy prospect of squaring up to the defending champions without his two best players.

Benitez had never beaten United in a Premier League game and his prospects would clearly not be improved if his two star men were forced to sit the match out. In fact, so poor was Liverpool's record under Benitez against the men from Old Trafford that they had failed even to score a goal against them in the past four years – and, on the one occasion when they did manage to breach the defence of their bitter rivals, it was thanks only to an own-goal by John O'Shea in a 2–1 defeat in September 2004.

So the task facing Liverpool, with or without Gerrard and Torres, was huge. Former goalscoring hero Ian Rush, however, was confident that the Reds could prevail on their home patch. He told the club's website, 'We've got to be confident because if you aren't then you won't get a result. We haven't started the season very well in terms of performances but we've got seven points on the board. If we can put the pressure on them [United], I think we can then start believing we can do something.

'We are three points ahead of Manchester United, and, although they have got a game in hand, if we can beat them we will be six points ahead. For the first time in a long time, they would be playing catch up to us. It's normally the other way around when we have to beat United to keep in contention.'

That confidence, clearly born out of winning when not playing at their best, was backed up by full-back Alvaro Arbeloa who was also bullish about his side's hopes of upsetting United, even allowing for the absence of their star duo. 'Fernando and Stevie are really important for us and they are probably our best players,' Arbeloa told liverpoolfc.tv. 'But we have a really good squad and know we have other really good players, too. We can still beat Manchester United without Fernando and Stevie.'

Whatever the bold words being spoken, however, the undoubted truth was that everyone in the red half of Merseyside wanted the pair involved against United. And the good news from behind the scenes was that both Torres and Gerrard were recovering well from their injuries and were working hard with the club's medical staff. And Benitez had certainly not given up hope of the pair proving their fitness before the big clash.

With just four days to go before the kick-off, the Anfield boss was still talking in encouraging terms of the two of them being available to face their huge rivals and, unsurprisingly, he was prepared to wait until the last possible moment before deciding on their fitness. In the end, on the day before kick-off, Benitez announced to the media that the pair had both won their respective fitness battles. He said, 'They are both much better. They came through a full training session this morning. It wasn't a very hard session, but they will both be in the squad. If they are in the squad, then they can play.

'It's important for us to have these two players of quality who can change a game. I'm not surprised they are available because the medical staff have done a good job and the players have been working really hard with the physios to get fit.'

Although both fit, their lack of match practice was clearly a concern for the Anfield chief and, when the teams were announced shortly before kick-off, both Torres and Gerrard were among Liverpool's substitutes. And barely had they taken their places on the bench when Manchester United opened the scoring as Liverpool made the worst possible start to the game.

United new boy Dimitar Berbatov found space on the right-hand side of the penalty area and his ball pulled back across the face of goal fell perfectly into the path of Carlos Tevez. The Argentine ace didn't need a second invitation and he dispatched his shot with aplomb into the top corner.

That early setback could easily have knocked Liverpool completely out of their stride, but they responded in style, and it took them just a little over 20 minutes to force an equaliser when Xabi Alonso's cross was palmed by Edwin van der Sar into the shins of defender Wes Brown. To the horror of United's defence – and to the delight of the vast majority of the Anfield crowd – the ball rebounded off Brown and into the net to level the scores.

But, although Liverpool could finally celebrate a first goal against United for four years, the fact that it was another own-goal meant that unwanted record of no Liverpool player scoring for them under Benitez remained intact. Fortunately, however, that particular jinx was soon to be lifted. With just 13 minutes left, Javier Mascherano's determination to win the ball high up the pitch gave Dirk Kuyt the opportunity to cross for substitute Ryan Babel and the young Dutchman gleefully tucked the chance into the roof of the net to send the Kop into raptures.

There was little to trouble Liverpool's defence in the closing minutes, and instead there was more misery for United as central defender Nemanja Vidic was sent off after collecting a second yellow card for leading with an elbow in a challenge on Alonso.

Liverpool's fans reacted joyously at the final whistle, and Benitez, too, was delighted with the result. He said, 'I think we can be really satisfied because we were losing against a top team. It is good for the confidence of the players. At half-time, we were talking about having confidence and determination going forwards – and in the second half we were the best team. We showed quality and character to come back.

'We didn't make many mistakes. We can always improve and do things better, but the team played well. One thing that we needed to improve was our results against the top sides so now we have three points and we are in a better position than last season.'

Defender Jamie Carragher, captain in the absence of Gerrard, was also thrilled with the win and called on his team-mates to use the three points as a springboard to go on and achieve success for the remainder of the season. 'It gives us belief and confidence because we've beaten the best team in Europe,' said Carragher. 'It gives us the belief that we can beat anyone in the league. We hope we can now push on for the rest of the season. It should spur us on, because we've not been playing too well. That is the best we've played. It also gives us a bit of breathing space between us and United, and top is where a club like Liverpool should be.'

Victory over United was the perfect fillip as the Reds prepared to begin their Champions League campaign in France against Marseille. Benitez added, 'We could not have asked for a better boost to our confidence than a victory over the best team in England, and the European Champions. Now we will go to Marseille in a good frame of mind. That was our best performance of the season and we now feel we can go into a Champions League game in good heart and spirit.

'We are still unbeaten, but we had not been at our best. The victory against Manchester United has changed all that. We have made a statement about our form in domestic competition, and the victory will not go unnoticed in Europe. We did it without Torres and Gerrard, and we will have to wait and see how they are for Europe. We have a few training sessions now before the game in France, and both of them have been improving all the time.'

A further confidence boost for Liverpool ahead of the trip to the south of France was the knowledge that they had beaten Marseille 4–0 at their intimidating Stade Velodrome home in a must-win encounter to book their place in last season's knockout stages. And on the eve of the match, Carragher revealed how he and his team-mates were dreaming of another final appearance in the Champions League, this time in Rome's Olympic Stadium, the scene of Liverpool's victories in the European Cup in both 1977 and 1984. He said, 'The club has great memories of Rome. Obviously, that's where it all started for us in the European Cup in 1977, and we then beat Roma on penalties in the final of the 1984 competition. That was a great achievement, so hopefully we can continue our history with Rome. It would be great to win another European Cup.'

And Carragher also admitted that he expected English clubs to dominate the Champions League again, just as they had done last season when three Premier League teams reached the semi-finals, with Chelsea and Manchester United eventually contesting the final. 'I just think that all the best players in the world are in this country [England],' added the combative defender. 'Look at Manchester City, who have just bought Robinho from Real Madrid – one of the biggest clubs in the world – when they're probably not one of the biggest clubs in England. That just shows the quality of talent in the Premier League.'

Midfielder Xabi Alonso was also confident that his team were displaying the necessary qualities to once more win in Marseille. He said, 'We know it will be a tough game because Marseille are a good side and they are playing well at the moment. But we will go there with confidence that we can get a result again.

'We will be looking to win the game because we know how important it can be to get three points on the board from your first game. If we do that then it makes things a little bit easier for us because we will have more confidence.'

Meanwhile, Marseille manager Eric Gerets, while insisting his players would not suffer a similar humiliation to that inflicted upon them almost 12 months previously, was a concerned man ahead of the season's Champions League opener. He said, 'Liverpool won't surprise us like last time. Their physical qualities hurt us a lot, but that won't happen this season. We won't make the same mistakes. But I am not reassured when I see how Liverpool played against Manchester United. That was impressive. I love watching football at that pace. Liverpool are like the Duracell bunnies – they are an example to the rest of the world for the effort they put in. You just wind them up and off they go.'

Quite what Liverpool's star names thought about being described as 'Duracell bunnies' is not a matter of record, but they did display the dogged determination Gerets appeared to be referring to by recovering from a one-goal deficit to record a magnificent 2–1 win on the night.

Both Torres and Gerrard were restored to the starting line-up following their injury lay-offs, and it was Gerrard who stole the show with both his side's goals, the first of which was an outrageous 30-yard curler that left the Marseille goalkeeper clutching desperately at thin air. It meant the perfect start for Liverpool in their quest to reach yet another Champions League final, and maintained their unbeaten start to the season. Not that manager Benitez was entirely satisfied. He said, 'We have plenty of room for improvement. The key was to get a third goal and finish the game. When we couldn't do that we were a bit lucky in the end. Coming from behind tells me we need to improve in defence but also that the mentality is very good.

'We are ready for winning and recovering from bad situations. The first game in your group is really important to win. It puts us in a good position. PSV and Atletico Madrid will find it difficult here.'

Gerrard also felt the side could have played better, adding, 'My first goal was a good finish but the real heroes were Pepe Reina and the back four. We came under pressure and we will look back at the tape of the second half to see where we went wrong because we did not pass the ball well.'

Perhaps the performance had not been out of the top drawer, but the result certainly was. And, in the opening exchanges in the Champions League, winning is clearly the key. But lingering doubts about the quality of the display and the side's form as a unit resurfaced just a few days later when Stoke visited Anfield in the Premier League. In the bad old days, this would have been one of those matches – against a supposed minnow – that Liverpool sides would have struggled with. Sadly, the bad old days made an unexpected return.

Admittedly, Liverpool were not helped by the decision of referee Andre Mariner to rule out Steven Gerrard's second-minute free-kick for an offside offence that no one else in the ground – or on the TV replays – could see, but they still had 24 shots on goal and failed to register with any of them.

It meant a disappointing 0–0 draw and the loss of two important home points as Stoke's blanket defence succeeded in shutting out the Reds. Manager Benitez admitted, 'It was impossible to create clear chances with all of their players inside the box. For a striker close to the box, it's especially difficult.'

That last comment could be viewed as a defence of Torres and Robbie Keane, who had managed just one Premier League goal between them in the side's first five games. Benitez, though, was convinced his newly formed strike pair would come good. 'Torres returned from the Euros a month later than normal and will need more time to build up his strength and fitness. Physically, he needs to improve,' said the Anfield boss. 'That doesn't help, but there were other problems against Stoke because he had no space and was under pressure all the time.

'Confidence becomes an issue with any striker when he is not scoring and it is clear Torres and Keane both need a goal. When it happens you will see a real difference.'

And the pair were also backed by fellow front-runners Dirk Kuyt and Albert Riera, who both insisted it was only a matter of time before the goals started to flow. 'The goals will come for Fernando and Robbie,' Kuyt said defiantly. 'We have no worries about that.'

And new boy Riera, signed on transfer-deadline day from

Espanyol, also had words of encouragement for his Spanish international colleague and his new partner. He said, 'I've known Fernando for a long time and every player has periods when they don't score – but they [Torres and Keane] are fantastic players. I'm sure they will score a lot of goals.'

For Keane, the pressure was surely greater, as Torres had more than proved his worth in his first season at the club and there was no doubt he would find his goalscoring boots again sooner rather than later. Keane, however, had a £20m price tag to live up to, but Torres was convinced he would soon start to repay that enormous outlay. He claimed, 'I know Robbie is going to be a very important player for us. Maybe he needs to score his first goal then he'll go on to score a lot more – as that's the type of player he is. When you arrive, you want to score straight away to relieve the pressure. He's just waiting to score that first goal but he's still great to have in the dressing room.'

It would have been of no small comfort to Keane to hear his partner and his other team-mates talking in glowing terms about him. And Torres also revealed that he drew his own inspiration from words spoken to him by Spanish legend Raul following Spain's early exit from the 2006 World Cup. 'When Spain went out of the World Cup, I was looking to Raul for comfort as one of the leaders of the team,' said Fernando. 'He just said [to me] to make sure I never felt like that again. It seemed harsh at the time but now I understand. Now, when we play games like the win against Manchester United, I remember how it was in the dressing room that day and I do everything I can not to feel like that again.'

Liverpool were able to get the disappointment of that Stoke stalemate out of their system with a 2–1 midweek Carling Cup victory over Crewe, a win that set them up perfectly for their next big Premier League test – the first Merseyside derby of the season at Goodison Park.

Liverpool had done the double over Everton in the previous season and Rafael Benitez was hoping for a similar outcome this time around. 'I have very good memories of the derby,' Benitez told the media in the build-up to the game. 'It is really important for the fans when you beat your rival in the derby, so I was really pleased last season. We won with a penalty in the last minute when we played them away last time, so we were happy.

'This game is more difficult [than others] because of the rivalry between the fans, but at the end of the day we are talking about just three points. The only difference is that during the week you can see that the fans are really happy you have won.'

Torres had been forced to sit out the previous season's Goodison encounter because of injury but he was fit and raring to go this time around. He had played the final 20 minutes of the win over Crewe, with Benitez admitting he was 'keen to give Fernando a run out', and there were signs he was beginning to discover his sharpness again after a relatively sluggish start to the season. And the signs of that sharpness were evident for all to see against Liverpool's local rivals as Torres doubled his tally for the season in one game with both goals in an excellent 2–0 win for the Reds.

His first came 12 minutes after half-time when he volleyed home Robbie Keane's superb pinpoint cross and he made the points safe just four minutes later when he pounced on a loose ball in the area to rifle his shot into the roof of the net.

They were his first goals since the opening-day victory at Sunderland and, although no one in the Anfield camp ever had any doubts that it was only a matter of time before he started scoring again, manager Benitez admitted that ending his drought would be good for both the player and the team. He said, 'It was important for Fernando and us that he started scoring, so to get two in a derby is massive for him. Clearly, Fernando is a player who can change games and it is positive that he has confidence now. He is always a threat to defenders and the only thing he is missing at the moment is his physical condition. When he came back from the European Championship, it was important for him to rest and then train properly. He had an injury and he still has to improve physically. He is working so hard and he will get better – he will have more pace and be stronger. Fernando knows he can still improve a lot and the main thing for me is that his mentality is really good. He scored 33 last season but I haven't set him a target this season. If he scores 32 I will be pleased!'

That win meant Liverpool ended the weekend level with Chelsea at the top of the table, and Benitez added, 'I am really pleased and I hope we can stay there for a long time. We can talk about the next game with more confidence. We have confidence and you can see the team is playing well and has a good balance. We are strong in defence and we know we can create in attack, so that is very important. When we are playing well, we know we can beat anyone.'

Torres, meanwhile, was delighted with his derby double but he was quick to share the praise with his fellow front-runners Keane and Dirk Kuyt, who played crucial roles in both of his match-winning strikes. He said, 'It is very simple – without Robbie and Dirk, the goals I scored would not have been created. They were involved in both goals and it is because they give everything for the team that I was able to score them.

'If you look at my first goal, the ball that Robbie crossed in was perfect and so was the run by Dirk which took the Everton defenders away and gave me a clear chance [to score the second goal]. It is always nice to score, but without my team-mates it would not have been possible.'

And Torres had further words of encouragement for Keane, who was still awaiting his first goal in a Liverpool shirt. The Spaniard added, 'It is not always easy to form a new partnership but we are working hard in training all the time and it was good to see that work pay off on Saturday. Robbie was very important for our victory and I am sure that very soon it will be him who is getting the goals because he is a great player. Once he gets his first goal, even more will follow because sometimes you just need to relieve the pressure with one goal.'

Torres had relieved any pressure that he might have been feeling over his lack of goals but he admitted that six blank games was too much of a barren run. 'Not scoring for six games is too long for a striker,' he said. 'But it hasn't been affecting my confidence because I knew that if I kept working hard the goals would arrive. Now I want to keep going and score again in the Champions League next week. I want to improve on my 33 goals from last season. It was an important three points. We know how important this game is for the fans and the players because we want to stay towards the top of the table. We know if we're in the top three or four in January, and also in the next round of the Champions League, then we can have a fantastic season.'

For now, however, he was happy simply to bask in the glory of another derby victory, particularly as he was fully aware of what it meant for the fans in terms of local bragging rights. 'I am so pleased for the staff, for the boss and for all the players,' he continued. 'But also for the workers in the factories, the offices, the restaurants, the hotels and the bars who want to win this game so much. I would like to dedicate my goals to them as thanks for their support. I hope we made them happy by winning. When we win, we win together – so this victory is shared between all of us. It is not about one player.'

Liverpool's excellent start to the season was a welcome boost to all at Anfield who were wary of the threat of falling behind the leaders early on, and it appeared as though it had prompted a radical change in Benitez's thinking. He had been widely criticised in many quarters for his rotation policy, but it looked as though he had softened on that approach towards the end of last season when the likes of Torres, Gerrard and Carragher were regularly picked in the starting line-up. And now, as the Reds prepared to face PSV Eindhoven in their second Champions League group game, he admitted for probably the first time that his thought process had been altered by the form of his first-choice players.

'I won't make many changes [for the PSV game]. If some players are on fire, maybe it is a good moment to keep them playing,' he told the media. 'Normally, we try to check how the players are physically, mentally and also how the team is tactically – and then we decide whether we will change more or less players. But now we are in a good position so I do not think that I will change too many. When some players are playing well, but are tired, you say, "OK, maybe we will have to keep them in." But then you play them, they are tired and you have to change them in a game. You never know. If you win, you can say, "OK, fantastic decision," but I don't think I will change too many players.

'When we were analysing things this week we knew we had four days between the Everton match and this one and four days between this match and the Manchester City game. Three days is not enough, four days is better.'

Benitez's players clearly felt a four-day break between the Everton and PSV games was plenty as they turned on the style against the Dutchmen to win 3–1. It was a terrific victory, notable for two memorable goals. Robbie Keane finally netted his first in a Liverpool shirt, while Steven Gerrard celebrated his 100th, a remarkable tally for a midfielder and one that makes him only the 16th player in the club's history to reach his ton.

Dirk Kuyt was the other scorer on a comfortable night for Liverpool that ended with them level on top of the group with Atletico Madrid, with both teams having taken the maximum six points from their first two games. And with their next two games against Atletico, firstly away and then at home, Benitez knew that a draw and a win from those matches would all but ensure qualification for the knockout stages. He said, 'We will go to Madrid and look to win. We know if we can get ten points we will be in a very good position to qualify.'

And the Anfield boss was in justifiably confident mood as he analysed the recent performances of his team. 'When you are winning big games in succession, when you are playing well, the confidence grows – especially when those games you have won include victories against Manchester United and Everton. The confidence is high and we aim to keep it that way. The wins over United and Everton have shown the team that they can beat anyone. Last season, people were saying we could not beat the top three, but we deserved to beat United and it was the same against Everton. Those wins show how much we have improved.'

That improvement continued in their next Premier League game, away at big-spending Manchester City, now hailed as the richest club in the world following their buy-out by the Abu Dhabi United group. Liverpool, though, had to do it the hard way to claim another three points. They found themselves two behind at half-time at the City of Manchester Stadium, trailing to goals from Stephen Ireland and Javier Garrido and facing a real test of their title credentials in the second half. That they recovered to win 3–2 says everything about the side's spirit and suggested that, at long last, they had found the key to consistency in the Premier League.

Torres started the comeback in the 55th minute as he again etched his name in the club's record books, this time as the scorer of Liverpool's 1,000th Premier League goal. It wasn't long before he made it 1,001 before Kuyt sealed victory in the very last minute.

It was a fightback and a result that thrilled Benitez, as did, once again, the performance of Torres. The Anfield boss said, 'We know how important Torres is. He cost us a lot of money but we knew we were signing a young player who could improve. His value is higher now. He was a good signing in every sense. I would not want to swap Fernando with anyone else in the world because he is my player and I'm very pleased with him. There are good players in Europe and all the way around the world, but better than Torres? No.

'I do not want to put a price on him because people will think I want to sell him and that is not the case, so I will not say any price. I'm sure all the players have a value, but not Torres. He is priceless to us. He is unbuyable.'

Those two goals at Eastlands took Torres' league total for Liverpool to 29, making him the club's top foreign scorer in the Premier League, overtaking Patrik Berger's previous best of 28. Even more impressive is the fact that Torres reached his total in just 39 games, while Berger, admittedly mostly from a wide position, took 148 games to accrue his tally.

But, just when it seemed all was going so well for both player and club, Torres suffered another setback – once again returning from international duty with an injury, the third time that had happened in just 18 months. He was forced to limp out of Spain's 2–1 World Cup-qualifying win over Belgium with a hamstring strain after just 16 minutes, and early indications suggested he would be sidelined for a minimum of ten days, ruling him out of Liverpool's Premier League meetings with Wigan and Chelsea and, heartbreakingly for Fernando himself, the Champions League trip to face Atletico Madrid.

For manager Benitez, however, the personal disappointment of his Spanish superstar was simply a small part of the equation. The longer-term damage his absence could do to the Reds' season was the real concern for the Anfield boss, who once more voiced his displeasure at losing key men following international trips.

His mood was not helped by seeing Ryan Babel join Torres on the treatment table after he picked up an ankle injury while playing for Holland against Norway. Benitez complained, 'I am very disappointed about this because it now looks like we will lose Fernando for three very important games. There are too many international games and the demands on the players are too much. Someone needs to analyse this situation because it is putting the players at risk of injury.

'Maybe the answer is for there to be a two-tier qualifying system because there are too many games in the qualifiers for the World Cup and the European Championship which are not competitive but which still place great demands on the players. These fixtures are unnecessary and maybe it would be better if the weaker countries played one another and the best of them went on to play the stronger countries in the qualifiers.'

Whatever Benitez's solutions to solve the problem of losing players to international duty, and the subsequent injury risks involved, however, the simple truth was that he would now have to make do without his star striker for probably the next couple of weeks. It meant a reshuffle for the game against Wigan, with Dirk Kuyt switching to a central attacking position alongside Robbie Keane. And, although Liverpool were again given a scare, trailing by both 1–0 and 2–1 at different times in the match, they recovered once again to win 3–2, with Kuyt netting twice, including the winner five minutes from time.

Remarkably, it was the fifth time already that Liverpool had come from behind to win a match in the season so far. But Steven Gerrard was quick to warn his team-mates that they couldn't keep gifting leads to their opponents. 'In the past few weeks, we have proved that you can never count us out in any situation, and the battling qualities we have shown are very important,' he said in the *Daily Mirror*. 'But we know that we cannot keep conceding the lead in games like we have done in the last two matches. Sooner or later, it is going to catch up with us, and we'll pay the price.

'We have shown the grit, determination and belief that there is in this squad this season, but we have to start dictating games. However, we are full of confidence after what we have achieved, and we believe that there is a lot more to come from this side than we have seen so far. We are ready to take it on to another level and the confidence we now have will help us.'

They would certainly have expected to need to find another gear for their next challenge – an away trip to Atletico Madrid in the Champions League, a journey they would have to make without the injured Torres, denying the striker a dream return to his former club.

At one stage, however, it looked as though it was not just Torres who would miss out on playing at the Vicente Calderon. Just a week before the match was due to take place, UEFA ruled that the game would have to be played at a neutral venue at least 300km from Madrid after the club were punished for incidents of crowd unrest and racism during their previous Champions League match at home to Marseille, and ordered to play their next two 'home' games in the competition away from the city. It was a decision Liverpool were unhappy with given the logistical problems it would cause their own supporters who had already made travel plans for the visit and, after Madrid decided to appeal the decision, UEFA ruled that the match could, in fact, be played at Atletico's home stadium.

Torres was subsequently offered a VIP seat in the stadium by Atletico president Enrique Cerezo in recognition of the huge part he had played in the club's recent history but, after consultation with the Anfield medical staff, it was decided that he would not make the trip to Madrid at all.

So, as his team-mates jetted off for their latest Champions League challenge, Torres was left to reflect on a missed opportunity to play once more at the stadium he loved so much. 'To not be in the Calderon for this match is a huge disappointment,' he said on his website. 'It was very special for me to be able to play this game, but unfortunately it is not to be. I want to thank Atletico Madrid for their invitation. I'm sorry for the fans, but after meeting with the coach, the medical staff and the physiotherapists, we have decided that it was best for me to remain in Liverpool because I would have lost virtually two days of recuperation. At this stage, we cannot afford ourselves this luxury.'

Sadly, all too experienced now with these types of injury, Torres was painfully aware that patience was the key to his recovery. All he do could as his team-mates headed for Spain was to concentrate on completing the daily rehabilitation schedule the Liverpool medical staff had created for him. As for the game itself, he knew that, with both sides having taken maximum points from their two group games, the winners would all but book themselves a place in the second phase of the competition.

He knew, of course, how hard it would be for Liverpool at the ground he had called home for so long, but was confident the Reds could return with all three points. He had also made it clear in the past that his wish was for both his current team and his former one to reach the last 16. 'We are both on track', he added. 'Now all that remains is to finish it off.'

But, while Torres was facing up to the disappointment of missing the Madrid trip as he recuperated from his latest injury, he did at least receive the boost of a nomination for one of football's most prestigious individual awards. Along with his Anfield team-mate Steven Gerrard, he was among the 30 names nominated for the coveted Ballon d'Or, the European Footballer of the Year trophy. Organised by *France Football* magazine, the award was inaugurated in 1956 and is recognised as being one of the most prestigious individual honours in the world game. Torres was very much in the running to be the 2008 recipient, with many leading experts predicting he was the favourite to take the trophy following his extraordinary exploits in his debut season at Anfield and his match-winning display in the final of Euro 2008.

The hugely respected *L'Equipe* newspaper in France, which indeed did make Torres the favourite for the award, stated, 'The "Kid" has become the best of forwards. Torres was decisive in the European Championship final, finishing a brilliant piece of skill with a clinical finish to earn Spain the title. The trophy is his first in professional football and comes on the back of a perfect year at Liverpool with 33 goals to his name, and a Champions League semi-final. The most expensive Spanish footballer ever deserves gold.'

Were he to take the award he would be the first Spanish recipient since the legendary Luis Saurez and, not surprisingly, his countrymen were backing him to achieve that accolade. And one man lending his voice to Torres' cause was the last Spaniard to score a winning goal in a major final. Marcelino netted the winner for his country in their 2–1 win over the Soviet Union in the 1964 European Championship final and he was a firm advocate of the Liverpool striker's claims to be crowned the best player in Europe. Marcelino told Spanish sports newspaper *As*, 'An important footballing nation like Spain needed another goal like the one I scored. Spain has world-class players, but Torres is the best. Nobody deserves the Ballon d'Or more, and this is coming from a goalscorer.

'With all due respect to the other candidates, I would give the award to Fernando Torres because he scored the winning goal in a European Championship final. Everyone in the side was outstanding, but he scored the wonder goal. It was a real striker's goal, because he did not just poke the ball home. He outstripped the defender for pace and beat the keeper with a great piece of skill. The goal belongs to the team, but it carries the mark of Torres and we have to take our hat off to him.'

His fellow Spaniards in the Liverpool squad – Pepe Reina, Albert Riera and Alvaro Arbeloa – were also backing Fernando to claim the prize, as was his club manager Rafael Benitez. The Anfield chief told the club's website, 'It's fair that Torres and Gerrard are there [among the nominees] because both players have been really good – in Gerrard's case for years, and Fernando was amazing last season. Both deserve to be there.

'Torres scored a lot of goals in his first season in the Premier League and after that scored the winner in the final of Euro 2008. Clearly, Cristiano Ronaldo and Xavi from Spain deserve to be up there as well. But, for me, it's between Ronaldo and Torres this season.'

In Torres' absence in Madrid, it was left to Robbie Keane to lead the line on his own and the Irishman performed admirably as the Reds maintained their unbeaten start to their Champions League campaign, and indeed their unbeaten start to the season. A confident opening in the Vicente Calderon saw Keane give the visitors a 14th-minute lead and they had several chances to increase their advantage and kill off the game. They failed to do so, however, and were made to pay for their profligacy when Portuguese winger Simao levelled the scores with just seven minutes left.

Manager Benitez was left to rue those missed opportunities and he certainly felt his side should have made the game safe long before Madrid's equaliser but, with seven points out of a possible nine in the group so far, they were well on course to qualify for the knockout stages. Indeed, the fact that they achieved such a good result away from home without Torres will have given them great heart, particularly as they faced up to the prospect of a visit to Stamford Bridge without their star front-runner.

Just as he was forced to sit out the previous season's trip to west London to face Chelsea with a hamstring injury sustained on international duty, so he would again. It was a cruel repetition of fate for both player and club. And with the two teams locked together at the top of the table it represented a real blow to Liverpool's hopes of winning at Stamford Bridge and opening up a three-point gap at the top of the Premier League. Recent history, after all, was hardly on their side. They had failed to score a single Premier League goal at Stamford Bridge under Benitez and that was obviously their first target as they attempted to become the first team to beat Chelsea at home for four years and eight months, an astonishing run of 86 unbeaten matches.

So it was clear that the absence of Torres would be felt heavily. Not that Benitez was feeling unduly sorry for himself as he approached the big clash, insisting that even without the Spaniard his side had the necessary firepower to cause an upset. He told the media on the eve of the match, 'I think we can beat Chelsea without Torres. I think we have enough quality. We have new players with a very good mentality and a lot of confidence, so I think we have enough to beat a very good team like Chelsea. We will go to Stamford Bridge to try to win and, if we do, perfect. If not, we'll try not to lose and that will still be positive because we'll still be unbeaten.'

Benitez called on his players to produce the 'perfect 90 minutes' and, while they did not quite live up to that lofty level of expectation, they were not too far away as they did indeed inflict Chelsea's first home defeat for almost five years, and the first for new manager Luiz Felipe Scolari.

The game was not a classic but it was a tightly fought battle and Liverpool enjoyed long spells of supremacy and were worthy winners courtesy of Xabi Alonso's 11th-minute goal which deflected past goalkeeper Petr Cech via defender José Bosingwa. Not that Alonso was interested in hearing any talk of it being an own-goal. He insisted, 'It was my goal. The shot was on its way towards the goal when it was deflected but that happens, that's part of football and you have to cope with these things when they go for you and when they go against you.

'I could have had a second goal as well when the ball hit the post [from a free-kick] but the main thing is to get the three points. It was very important for us because in the last few seasons in the league we have been coming here and we haven't had the best results. So we are really pleased to get the result and to take the three points. We always believed that we could win here but we knew we would have to work really hard and we knew it would be very tough. In the first half, especially, it was really difficult because they played really good football and we were having a few problems trying to cope with their movement. But in the second half we were much better and we were able to control the game much better, even though we did not make the most of a couple of chances we had to score the second goal that would have killed the game. It's a great victory but it is only three points. The three points against Chelsea are as important as the three points against Wigan – they are all of the same value.'

It is true, of course, that all wins carry the same numerical value in terms of points but this victory sent a clear message to the rest of the Premier League that Liverpool intended to be around for the long haul this season. In previous years, their results against the three other members of the 'Big Four' had been their Achilles heel and a major reason why they had always fallen away. This season already, however, they could point to victories over both Manchester United and Chelsea as irrefutable evidence of their improvement. Add to that the resilience they had shown to bounce back late on to claim vital wins against Middlesbrough, Manchester City and Wigan, and it was clear that this was a very different Liverpool to that of recent memory.

After overseeing the team's best ever start to a Premier League season, that was a point Benitez was not shy of making to reporters following victory at Stamford Bridge. He insisted, 'We have the quality and the mentality to fight against the top sides and anyone else. To win at Stamford Bridge was a really difficult thing to do and it sends a massive message to the other teams of what we can do and tells our fans what we are about. We can go to any stadium and win games. Here, against a very good team, a very offensive team, we showed we were thinking about winning. The players know what to do. We have belief, we have quality, we showed coming from behind in the other games that we had character. Everybody was talking about statistics and our record against the top sides and we knew they were unbeaten at home for a long time, so it was a massive game for us.'

And Benitez also admitted that he was thrilled to see his side cope again without Torres as further evidence that they were not over-reliant on the Spaniard's goals. Indeed, he could point to the fact that they had now beaten both Manchester United and Chelsea without the injured star. Not that he would want to make a habit of seeing his main striker on the sidelines, of course. But he did admit,

'Everybody was talking about how it would be difficult for us to come to Chelsea without Torres. Fernando is a key player for us who can change a game and is always a threat for the defenders. But, if you work well as a team together you can manage like we showed [against Chelsea]. If we have to play one or two more games without Fernando, I think we have enough quality in the squad.'

The next challenge for Liverpool was to back up that magnificent win against Chelsea with victory over Portsmouth in their next game just three days later. And Benitez was aware that the critics would be looking to see if his side could do that after they had slipped up against struggling Stoke in the match immediately following their triumph over Manchester United earlier in the campaign. He added, 'We must start thinking about Portsmouth. We know we need to get three points against them if we want to keep with this mentality and momentum. After all, we were criticised for beating Manchester United and then drawing with Stoke so we have to be different now. Clearly, if you want to stay at the top of the table for a long time, you have to beat almost everyone because Chelsea, United and Arsenal will be behind you.'

And the Anfield manager even went so far as to admit that, if his side were to be crowned champions for the first time in almost two decades, they would need a near-perfect season to achieve it. He said, 'You can talk about maybe needing 95 points which was what Chelsea got [in 2004/05] or 92, maybe 87, so you cannot lose too many games. That is the reason why it is more difficult. The top three teams don't lose many games, so if you want to win or even be close you have to keep winning a lot of games in a row. It has to be almost perfect if you want to be at the top of the table at the end of the season. Chelsea, Manchester United and Arsenal will not lose too many games. One of them might make mistakes, but three at the same time? It is very difficult.'

For the first time in a long time, Liverpool found themselves in a position to be shot at, sitting at the top of the table, and Benitez admitted that the pressure to maintain their current form was building from outside the club. But he refused to accept that his side might suffer in the race for the title because Liverpool's players were not used to being in the shake-up for the top prize come the end of the season. 'The mentality of the players is good,' he insisted. 'The problem will be – and it will be a good problem – if we continue winning two or three more games and we stay at the top of the table and everyone will talk about us being contenders and then we will have more pressure from outside. But we have people on the staff who have won titles – Sammy Lee, Mauricio Pellegrino and me as a manager. And the players have won the Champions League, which is a massive trophy, so we have the experience.'

And those claims that Liverpool could cope with the pressure of being early-season leaders, and perhaps even thrive on it, were backed up by Jamie Carragher, who insisted the club's place on top of the pile was merely where they should be. The defender insisted, 'We're not getting carried away at being top of the league after nine games. That's where we should be. We're a massive club with a lot of top players, so we're only doing what we should be doing. Being top of the league, we're now going to be the team people will look to beat. I'm sure people will talk about us more. We're going to have to deal with that now. But we've got a lot of experienced players, big internationals who have won trophies before. It's something we will have to handle.'

And handle it they did against Portsmouth, but only just. With manager Harry Redknapp having quit Fratton Park for Tottenham just a few days earlier, new boss Tony Adams set up his team at Anfield to make it as difficult as possible for Liverpool to break them down. And with Torres still sidelined, for a fourth successive game, it needed a 75th-minute penalty from Steven Gerrard to claim all three points and keep Liverpool ahead of Chelsea at the top of the table by the same margin.

It was far from a vintage performance by the Reds but Benitez insisted afterwards that the end result mattered far more than the overall display. And, after making four changes to the side that had won at Stamford Bridge, he insisted that it was a further demonstration to any remaining doubters that Liverpool now had the strength in depth in their squad to ensure they remained in the title race for the long haul this time. He said, 'This sends the message to the players and everyone that we can change it [the team] and still win. After the victory over Chelsea, winning this game was always going to be the main thing. We want to stay at the top for a long time.'

By a strange quirk of fate, their next challenge in their quest to remain at the head of the pack came against Redknapp's new side at White Hart Lane. And with the former West Ham boss clearly working his magic straight away, leading Spurs to a win and a draw in his first two games in charge, trebling their points tally for the season in the process, it was clear that Liverpool would face a real test in north London.

It was a test Torres had battled hard to be fit for but, on the eve of the match, Benitez revealed that his injury would once more force the side's star striker to miss the trip to the capital. 'Fernando is very close,' said Benitez. 'He is back in training and we want to get him back playing as soon as possible.'

The player himself was clearly becoming frustrated by what was now turning into a fairly length lay-off and the Anfield boss admitted that he and his staff were now having to protect Torres from himself. He admitted, 'If you ask him then he will say that he is ready, but I've spoken with the physios, the doctor and the fitness coach and we know we need to be careful with him. He could perhaps have played against Portsmouth but it would have been a big risk. We will decide nearer the time, but he could return against Atletico Madrid.'

A comeback against his former club was just the tonic Torres would have been hoping for and the game against the Spaniards, their second meeting in a fortnight, took on added significance for everyone at Anfield after their fantastic unbeaten start to the season came to an end at Spurs as they surrendered the last unblemished record in senior British football. The Reds looked on course to maintain their lead at the top of the table after Dirk Kuyt gave them the perfect start with the opening goal after just three minutes of the match at White Hart Lane. And it was a lead they should probably have trebled or even quadrupled as they totally dominated proceedings, particularly in a purple patch immediately after half-time.

A mixture of the woodwork and some profligate finishing, however, conspired to prevent them adding to the Dutchman's early goal and, as so often happens in football at the highest level, they were made to pay for those missed chances late on in the game.

Tottenham, in fairness, had scarcely threatened the Liverpool goal before Jamie Carragher headed past his own goalkeeper, Pepe Reina, from a corner with 20 minutes remaining. Bizarrely, it was the second own-goal of the defender's career against Spurs – ten years after the first one.

But, if that blow was not bad enough, the Anfield side were stunned in the final minute when substitute Roman Pavlyuchenko bundled the ball home from close range to give the home side an extremely unlikely three points, meaning it was a shell-shocked Rafael Benitez who faced the media afterwards. 'I can't believe we have lost this game,' he said. 'After playing well in the first half, we started the second half with four clear chances. We hit the bar and Kuyt and Alonso had great chances that we didn't take.

'It's always important to create chances but you have to score from them. We were going forward, controlling the game and were dominant. I am really disappointed. It was really bad luck because everybody could see we were better than them. We could have won 4–0, but we need to take our chances.'

On a positive note for his side, though, Benitez revealed that Torres was expected to be fit to play a part against Madrid. 'Hopefully he will be ready,' added the Reds' chief. 'If he cannot start the game, then he will be on the bench if everything is OK.'

With the game so important to Torres for emotional reasons,

however, particularly after he missed the game in Madrid two weeks previously, Benitez added a note of caution by warning that he would be extra vigilant when determining the striker's fitness. 'In a normal game, you would talk with a player, but in this game it is even more important that I talk to him because I'm sure that he will try and say, "Yes, I want to play,"' added Benitez. 'We have to decide if he is 100 per cent fit or not. Sometimes the players can be desperate to play, so you have to be careful, but, in this case, I think that he has some experience. I will talk with him and see how he feels. I would like to see him ready as soon as possible, that is very clear, but the team is playing well. Because it's his hamstring, he has to decide with his head and not his heart.'

Ultimately, whether the decision was made by the player, the coaching staff or the club's medical experts, head did once again rule heart and, when the teams were announced shortly before kick-off, Torres was once more conspicuous by his absence. It was a massive disappointment for him to miss out for a second time on a reunion with his former team-mates but, with the Spaniard having suffered hamstring injuries three times in the past 18 months while away on international duty, there was no chance of Liverpool taking a gamble with their prize asset. Benitez insisted, 'He has had the problem because he was doing different things [in training], but now we are talking with the fitness coach of the Spanish team, so we know what Fernando has to do. He is doing exercises to prevent the problem and we are trying to keep it under control.

'Spain changed their manager, so we have to keep in touch with them. The fitness coach was my fitness coach in the Real Madrid youth team, so we have a good relationship and the communication is really good. The problem with Torres is that he has done it twice previously with the national team and now a third time with a new staff, so we just have to check and control it a bit more.'

What it meant for Liverpool in the short term, of course, was a sixth consecutive match without Torres in their squad. He was given a terrific welcome by both sets of fans as he took his seat in the stands to watch his new team take on his old one, but could only watch in growing frustration as Liverpool wasted chance after chance against their Spanish visitors. Trailing to Maxi Rodriguez's first-half strike, the Reds bombarded Atletico's goal in the second period but couldn't find the equaliser they sought so desperately. A night that looked like ending in widespread frustration was summed up beautifully just moments before the end when central defender Daniel Agger headed a golden chance wide of the target from close range.

As the Anfield crowd joined in a collective groan of anguish, the television cameras panned to a face in the crowd who could be seen rolling his eyes skywards with a resigned look and then burying his head in his hands. It was a picture that spoke a thousand words as Torres revealed his disappointment. And to those watching, it was obvious that the Spaniard believed that had he been on the pitch, and the chance had fallen to him, the net would now be bulging.

In the end, in an extraordinary climax, Liverpool salvaged a point thanks to an injury-time equaliser from Steven Gerrard. The skipper himself was sent tumbling to the turf under a challenge from defender Mariano Pernia and Swedish referee Martin Hansson – with guidance from his assistant – had no hesitation in pointing to the penalty spot. In truth, it looked a soft penalty but very few people in the ground were complaining as Gerrard picked himself up to send goalkeeper Leo Franco the wrong way from the spot-kick.

So a second successive 1-1 draw between the group's joint leaders ensured they remained locked on eight points apiece at the head of the table. And with Marseille and PSV Eindhoven having swapped wins in their two back-to-back clashes, both Liverpool and Atletico now knew that a win for either of them in the next round of matches would book their place in the knockout stages.

And, for Liverpool, the point was important not only to maintain their chase for Champions League qualification, but also to prevent a second successive defeat that could have provoked a crisis of confidence within the squad. Goal hero Gerrard admitted, 'It was a big result for us and a big point. Good teams usually don't lose two games in a row and so it was important we got something.'

As for the penalty, the Anfield captain felt it was a deserved award, but confessed that he would have felt differently had it been given against him. 'In my mind, it was a penalty,' he stressed. 'I got there first and he came into the back of me. If it had happened anywhere else on the pitch it would be a free-kick, so it was a penalty. I can understand their disappointment because of the timing of it. If it had happened at the other end, we would have been livid. But that's football and we have to move on.'

It was another late, late rescue act by Liverpool against the Spaniards, demonstrating once more the resilience they had shown all season and their refusal to accept defeat or, in many cases, a draw. But what was becoming clear was that, although they were maintaining their form and their strong start to the season, they were missing a crucial cutting edge.

In the six games Torres had missed, Liverpool had scored just eight goals, and three of those came in the very first one against Wigan. Since then, they had managed just one goal a game in the next five and it was obvious they needed their talismanic striker back in the starting line-up.

He didn't quite make it into the first XI for the next match at home to West Brom in the Premier League but there was great relief all round that he was finally fit enough to take his place among the substitutes. And Benitez was afforded the perfect chance to reintroduce Torres into the fray as Liverpool established a comfortable 2–0 lead against West Brom, thanks to a brace from Robbie Keane, his first Premier League goals for the club, meaning the game was all but won with 20 minutes remaining and Fernando could enjoy a brief cameo without the need to overexert himself. He received a rapturous reception as he took to the field in place of Keane and, although he had little chance to make a real impact, he helped Liverpool secure the victory thanks to a wonderful third goal from Alvaro Arbeloa.

It was a huge boost for Benitez to welcome back his star striker and he was now looking forward to Torres playing a full part in the remainder of the season and taking some of the weight of expectation off the side's other star performers, particularly Gerrard. The pair had linked up so successfully throughout the previous season and Benitez was clearly looking forward to a resumption of that lethal combination, as well as Torres' partnership with Keane, which had started to develop along very promising lines before the Spaniard's injury.

The Anfield boss said, 'I think Gerrard's level will improve with Torres available. It is clear that Stevie is a bit tired at the moment but with Torres he will have another player who can benefit from the accuracy of his passing. And Torres will improve with fitness.'

In a bid to get some much-needed match fitness under his belt, Torres was included in what was very much a second-string Liverpool side to take on Tottenham in the Carling Cup at White Hart Lane, just 11 days after the north Londoners had inflicted the Reds' first defeat of the season upon them. And it was a trick they were to repeat in a 4–2 win in a worrying setback for Rafa Benitez that suggested that maybe his squad lacked strength in depth as some of the fringe players failed to take an opportunity to impress.

As for Torres, he, too, struggled to make a real impact on the game, not surprisingly perhaps considering the inadequacies of some of his team-mates. But the most important thing for him was that he played for almost an hour before being replaced by Emiliano Insua as he stepped up his comeback. And Benitez was confident that, now the hamstring injury was cleared up, once he got his strength back, Torres would be as good as ever, if not even better following his enforced lay-off. Benitez insisted, 'Having him back fitter and stronger than before can have a massive effect on this team and help Liverpool a great deal. It is true we were worried about his fitness when he came back after the summer and after such a long season he was not at his best level. But now he has had a rest and we are hoping to bring him back ready to play to his true level.

'We have managed to win in his absence and keep pace in the league and now we have Torres back fitter and stronger, so it has been a good period for us. When you consider that we have been getting good results without our players being at their top level, the return of Torres at his best can have a big impact.'

There was no doubt that was the case but Benitez was determined not to rush his star striker and risk further damage and so it was that he was once more named among the substitutes for the Premier League trip to Bolton as Liverpool looked to bounce back from that Carling Cup exit.

And they did so in fine style, winning 2–0 at the Reebok Stadium against one of the country's most combative teams in a fixture that has in the past caused Liverpool considerable problems.

But there were no such concerns on this occasion as goals from Dirk Kuyt and Steven Gerrard sealed a comfortable victory in a game that, if truth be told, Liverpool should have won by a far wider margin. There were no complaints from the Anfield camp, however, as they remained locked at the top of the Premier League with Chelsea. And, with a third of the season now gone, the question marks about Liverpool's capacity to last the distance were beginning to be removed.

Benitez had stated on Torres' return from injury that the Spaniard's presence would help Gerrard and there was evidence of that at Bolton as the pair began to rekindle the partnership that had blossomed so impressively the previous season. Indeed, it was Torres who provided the perfect ball for Gerrard to settle the match at the Reebok, delivering an exquisite cross with the outside of his right foot straight on to the onrushing midfielder's forehead. Gerrard duly dispatched a clinical header wide of goalkeeper Jussi Jasskelainen.

So with positive news all round, it was no surprise that the players and management at the club were beginning to view their title challenge more in expectation than hope as they continued their impressive start. Certainly, Torres had seen enough during his time on the sidelines to offer encouragement that the team were capable of delivering a first domestic title for 19 years. And, although he was far too modest to say it, the fans were certainly united in their thinking that, with the Spaniard back in the side, those chances were improved still further.

And there was a real, steely edge to Fernando's words as he looked forward to the rest of the campaign and stressed that winning the Premier League title was the priority of everybody at Anfield. Hailing Rafael Benitez as 'the best coach I have ever had, without doubt,' he continued. 'When I arrived at Liverpool, everyone talked about the league title. We have won it 18 times and Manchester United 17. If they win it this season, they will draw level and the fans don't want that.'

It was clear from those words that the players didn't want that either. And with Liverpool's number 9 back to full fitness and in determined mood, there was every chance they would prevent it. And whether or not that pursuit proved ultimately successful, there was no doubt that with Torres leading Liverpool's front line for the forseeable future, the Reds would be a genuine force to be reckoned with once more.